W9-BLV-424

Inside Islam

Inside Islam

A Guide for Catholics

Daniel Ali and Robert Spencer

Ascension Press
West Chester, Pennsylvania

Ascension Press, L.L.C.
Post Office Box 1990
West Chester, PA 19380
Orders: (800) 376–0520
www.AscensionPress.com

Cover design: Kinsey Caruth
Printed in the United States of America
03 04 05 06 9 8 7 6 5 4 3 2 1
ISBN 0–9659228–5–5

Contents

To my wife, Sara, and my parents — without them I would not be the person I am; to my friends Charles Jamison, David and Kyle Dibble (for all their encouragement), and Steve Epstein (with gratitude); and to the memory of the late Father William G. Most.

— Daniel Ali

To all those who seek the truth of Christ with sincere hearts.

— Robert Spencer

Abbreviations

Old Testament

Gn	Genesis	Jon	Jonah
Na	Nahum	Mi	Micah
Ex	Exodus	Hb	Habakkuk
Lv	Leviticus	Zep	Zephaniah
Nm	Numbers	Hg	Haggai
Dt	Deuteronomy	Zec	Zechariah
Jos	Joshua	Mal	Malachi
Jgs	Judges		
Ru	Ruth		
1 Sam	Samuel	**New Testament**	
2 Sam	2 Samuel	Mt	Matthew
1 Kgs	1 Kings	Mk	Mark
2 Kgs	2 Kings	Lk	Luke
1 Chr	1 Chronicles	Jn	John
2 Chr	2 Chronicles	Acts	Acts
Ezr	Ezra	Rom	Romans
Neh	Nehemiah	1 Cor	1 Corinthians
Tb	Tobit	2 Cor	2 Corinthians
Jdt	Judith	Gal	Galatians
Est	Esther	Eph	Ephesians
1 Mc	1 Maccabees	Phil	Philippians
2 Mc	2 Maccabees	Col	Colossians
Jb	Job	1 Thess	1 Thessalonians
Ps	Psalms	2 Thess	2 Thessalonians
Prv	Proverbs	1 Tm	1 Timothy
Eccl	Ecclesiastes	2 Tm	2 Timothy
Sng	Songs	Ti	Titus
Wis	Wisdom	Phlm	Philemon

Sir	Sirach	Heb	Hebrews
Is	Isaiah	Jas	James
Jer	Jeremiah	1 Pt	1 Peter
Lam	Lamentation	2 Pt	2 Peter
Bar	Baruch	1 Jn	1 John
Ez	Ezekiel	2 Jn	2 John
Dn	Daniel	3 Jn	3 John
Hos	Hosea	Jude	Jude
Jl	Joel	Rv	Revelation
Am	Amos	CCC =	*Catechism of*
Ob	Obadiah		*the Catholic Church*

Foreword

Islam glories in the clear simplicity of its doctrine and demands. The faith of the Muslim can be understood by the least educated person, and the religion offers a promise of eternal happiness in a paradise appealing to the senses. Muslims criticize Christianity for a number of reasons, but chief among them is that Christianity is too complex a mystery to be true. Furthermore, the belief in a heaven where the blessed see God face-to-face seems blasphemous to the Muslim.

Despite Islam's profession of a simple, clear faith, this religion is not well known to most Westerners. The media presents many news stories about Muslims without offering any real explanation of Islam and its tenets. Rarely does one encounter an article or program which explains the essential differences between secular Arab nationalism and Islamic religious movements. Many Western Christians remain unclear about the differences between the various Muslim sects: How do Sunni and Shiite differ? What are Wahhabi Muslims?

Since the conflicts in the Middle East have involved America in two wars and terrorism has inflicted horrors upon our own shores and abroad, the sale of the Koran in its English translation has greatly increased in the United States. Many American Christians want to better understand Islam but find that the more closely they approach this enigmatic faith, the more complex it seems. Since the Koran is not organized chronologically or thematically, it is difficult for the non-Muslim to make sense of it. The Koran appears so strange to Western eyes that many readers find it difficult to find a firm starting point to read it with comprehension.

Another problem in understanding Islam stems from the many conflicting ideas existing within it. Is it a religion of peace or a religion of warlike *jihad*? Does jihad mean the individual struggle to submit to God more completely or does it refer to the universal struggle against every non-Muslim society and structure? If Islam teaches so many good things about Jesus Christ and the Virgin Mary, why do Muslims have so many difficulties with Christian beliefs?

The committed Christian, then, is faced with a central question: Does the choice between Islam and Christianity make any difference in living life on earth or achieving eternal bliss in the next life? Both Islam and Christianity claim to be God's true revelation, so how does a Christian respond to Islam's claim? Is there a way to sift through the Koran, pull together its themes of revelation, and make sense of it from a Christian perspective? Though Muslims are actively seeking converts from among Christians, is it possible to evangelize Muslims about Christianity? How can one begin to discuss the issues which separate the two religions?

I commend the authors of this book for helping Catholics tackle this most important topic. They have presented many of the key beliefs of Islam in a clear question-and-answer format. Their deep insights into the text and language of the Koran are truly enriching, especially for the relatively new student of Islam.

Though unabashedly Christian, Daniel Ali and Robert Spencer have chosen to treat this world religion and its believers with the respect they are due. First, Muslims are recognized as persons who truly want to please God by submitting to Him, and their commitment and sincerity are respectfully presented. Second, a great wealth of information from Islamic sources — the Koran, Muhammad's Tradition (the

Hadith), and the opinions of Islamic scholars — is presented and discussed extensively, with source citations provided so that the reader can personally examine the texts. And third, they take the claims of Islam seriously, as is proper for a religion which has changed the lives of hundreds of millions over thirteen centuries and across many cultures. Islam claims a divine origin for its revelation, so its texts must be read from the point of view of such a high claim.

This respectful attitude towards Islam involves a process of serious, careful attention to the data of Islamic revelation. However, the authors also note the difficulties, tensions, and contradictions within the Islamic literature precisely because they take it so seriously. Daniel Ali had to face these difficulties personally — though once a believing Muslim, the tensions he began to see within Islam became such a weighty challenge that he was moved to increase his study of Islamic texts until he eventually came to accept that Jesus Christ is the true Son of God and Lord of all.

Having heard Mr. Ali speak many times, I am again deeply impressed at his brilliant insights into the many difficulties presented by the Koran. His deep understanding of its language and careful examination of the Arabic vocabulary help the non-Arabic-speaking Christian follow the arguments about its claims to be the reliable, perfect, inspired word of Allah. His co-author, Robert Spencer, also comes to the project with an extensive knowledge of the religion of Muhammad, having written two previous books on Islam. Mr. Spencer's background as a Catholic apologist and teacher have served this present book well.

Inside Islam: A Guide for Catholics is especially for those Christians who want to submit to Jesus' command to make disciples of all nations. This book is definitely not for the timid or indifferent Catholic. It is for those who truly want to explore the mystery that is Islam, so that they might be better prepared to proclaim the saving truth of Christ to their Muslim neighbors. No one who is beginning to confront the reality of Islam should be without this book. May God bless all who read it.

— Fr. Mitch Pacwa, S.J.

Introduction

Islam. To some, the word itself is frightening; to others, mysterious. Whether Islam evokes fear or intrigue, it has become increasingly clear that the modern Western world cannot afford to ignore this enigmatic religion. The terrorist attacks of September 11, 2001, the recent war with Iraq, and the ongoing crisis plaguing the Holy Land have put Islam in the news now more than ever. Nevertheless, most Catholics know little about this formidable faith — an ignorance that could have profound consequences for the future.

While the post-Christian West is afflicted with spiritual apathy and religious indifferentism, Islam is flourishing. Aside from high rates of immigration and rapid population growth, Islam is growing in the West mainly because it stands for something — it has clearly-enunciated beliefs and values. This can be very attractive to people living in a secular, skeptical age. In addition, as long as non-Muslims care little about understanding, explaining, or defending their own religious beliefs, Islam will stand unchallenged because the committed and practicing Muslim is always ready to share what he believes.

Some Christians might say, "Islam is growing. So what?" They might argue that Muslims believe in one God, the same God of Abraham that Jews and Christians worship. Catholics might add that the *Catechism of the Catholic Church* speaks of Muslims as somehow involved with the "plan of salvation" (CCC 841). In light of all this, does it really matter whether or not they are introduced to Christianity?

Yes, it most emphatically does.

Here's why: Although there are undoubtedly millions of

virtuous Muslims, Islam itself is an incomplete, misleading, and often downright false revelation which, in many ways, directly contradicts what God has revealed through the prophets of the Old Testament and through His Son Jesus Christ, the Word made flesh. And, as you will see in the coming pages, its beliefs have serious consequences for human dignity and the cultures of the countries in which it dominates. For several reasons (which many in the West have tried to ignore or explain away), Islam constitutes a threat to the world at large. Despite having agreement with Christianity on some fundamental beliefs, Islam's theology and its aggressive growth are not benign realities. Indeed, Christians ignore them at their own risk.

Islam is now embraced by more than a billion people — one out of every six people on the planet. At its current rate of growth, Islam could become the world's largest religious group in less than twenty years. Moreover, Islam for quite some time has not been confined to the Middle Eastern lands that Westerners most often associate with it. It now predominates in countries around the globe, and the majority of Muslims worldwide are not Arabs. Indeed, the largest Muslim nation on earth — Indonesia — is very far from the Middle East.

In recent years, Islam has grown rapidly in Europe — especially in such historically Christian nations as Germany and France — and in North America as well. The United States now has more Muslims than Presbyterians. Every month, new mosques are being established in all parts of the country, particularly in our major cities. The days when a Catholic would be as likely to meet a Muslim as he or she would a bushman of Africa are long gone. In all probability, the coming years will find many Catholics in the United States encountering followers of Islam in their neighborhoods, schools, and supermarkets. Catholics need an understanding of this mysterious faith so that they will be better prepared in this age of dialogue to counter its challenges to Christianity, and to be more effective witnesses to the Gospel.

Inside Islam: A Guide for Catholics utilizes a question-and-answer format so that all Catholics — both the theological novice and the well-catechized — can learn the basics of Islam. In most of the answers, the authors have provided the reader with an explanation of Catholic teaching on the topic at hand, so as to illustrate more clearly the deficiencies of many Islamic beliefs and at the same time to help you more fully grasp your Catholic faith. As far as we know, *Inside Islam* is the first question-and-answer book on Islam from a Catholic perspective in several decades.

To help you move through the book at a good pace, we have put extra information about many of Islam's intriguing beliefs in the back of the book as endnotes. You'll find many questions explored in greater depth there.

My co-author Daniel Ali is a Catholic convert from Islam. Raised in Iraq, Daniel was moved at a young age by the silent witness of charity and good moral lives of several Christians that his family always seemed to have as neighbors. When he was seven, one Christian neighbor gave him a cross, a gift which he cherished for the next eight years of his life. A student of history and philosophy, Daniel began an intense study of his Islamic faith, trying to answer the question of why his Muslim brothers in Northern Iraq did not seem to notice or care about the suffering, agony, and genocide of their Kurdish Muslim brothers. In time, his study led him to the foot of the Cross — to the realization that the God of the Universe does indeed desire an intimate relationship with man, and that He did, in fact, send His Son to dwell among us. In 1998, Daniel was received into the Catholic Church by Father William Most.

My own study of Islam began in 1980, when I first read the Koran at the invitation of Palestinian and Saudi Muslims who were trying to convert me. My interest in Islam was fueled by my family history: my grandparents, who were Christians, grew up among Muslims in the Ottoman Empire and came to the United States in 1919 as that empire was collapsing. I read widely in Muslim sources for two decades, and so was not surprised on September 11, 2001, when radical Islam brought death and ruin to our shores. In order to explain how core elements of Islam can have this kind of devastating impact on the spirit of humanity, I wrote *Islam Unveiled: Disturbing Questions About the World's Fastest Growing Faith* (San Francisco: Encounter Books, 2002), a book written for a secular audience and which quickly became a best-seller. I followed up that book with an in-depth study of jihad, *Onward Muslim Soldiers: How Jihad Still Threatens America and the West* (Washington, D.C.: Regnery Publishing, 2003). As a Christian, I take even greater satisfaction in the present book, because both Daniel and I believe it will be a powerful tool to equip Catholics to become better witnesses of their own faith to Muslims.

It is our sincere hope and prayer that you may experience the same intellectual and spiritual awakening Daniel and I experienced in our critical study of Islam, and that you may become a confident witness for our Savior Jesus Christ to those who embrace this challenging faith.

— Robert Spencer

Questions and Answers

1. What is Islam?

Islam is the religion of more than a billion people on earth — a far cry from its humble and obscure beginnings in seventh-century Arabia. Islam is the dominant faith in over fifty countries stretching from Morocco to Indonesia. It is generally classified as one of the three great monotheistic religions along with Judaism and Christianity, and it contains numerous ties to the Judeo-Christian tradition.

Muslims worship one God, *Allah*, and they revere the man they consider to have been His last and greatest prophet, Muhammad, a seventh-century Arabian.

2. I have heard that the number of Muslims is rapidly increasing each year throughout the world. Is this true?

Yes, it is. Islam is one of the fastest-growing religions in the world.

The main reason for this trend is population growth, though adult converts make up a significant portion of Islam's expansion as well. The number of Muslims in the world is increasing faster than the world population as a whole. In addition, those who proselytize for Islam are aggressive, well-prepared, and successful.

Islam is sweeping through Africa and gaining ground in former Catholic bastions such as the Philippines. In the West, a few high-profile converts — such as Muhammad Ali, Cat Stevens, Mike Tyson, Ahmad Rashad, and NBA stars

Kareem Abdul-Jabbar, Larry Johnson, Mahmood Abdul-Rauf, Tariq Abdul-Wahad, and Shareef Abdur-Rahim — have given Islam an aura of *cool*. In the United States there are now about as many Muslims as there are Jews — and more Muslims than Presbyterians. Over the past forty years, Islam has also made significant inroads among African Americans, as witnessed by the rise of the Nation of Islam and other black Muslim groups (although traditional Sunni and Shiite Muslims consider the Nation of Islam and similar sects to be heretical).

Far from suffering a drop-off after the September 11, 2001 terrorist attacks, Muslim groups have claimed a large influx of converts in the United States and Europe. Meanwhile, huge numbers of immigrants have given Islam the foothold in Europe that the warriors of *jihad* could never gain for it. In the Netherlands, France, and Germany, Muslims are becoming a political and religious force that cannot be ignored.

Even if population trends change, immigration stops, and Muslim missionary efforts cease, Islam looks to be significantly stronger worldwide in the new century than it has been in ages. While millions of Catholics have bought into the one- or two-child mentality of secular Europe and North America, Islamic societies are rapidly increasing in numbers. If current trends continue — and there is no reason to think that they will not — Europe will make up just 7.5 percent of the world's people by 2050, compared to 22 percent in 1950. At the same time, the countries with the most youthful populations will all be Muslim: Saudi Arabia, Pakistan, Afghanistan, Yemen, and Iraq. Worldwide trends indicate that by 2050, Muslims will comprise 30 percent of the world's population, with Christians (Catholic, Orthodox, and Protestant) making up 25 percent. In 1900, by comparison, only

12.4 percent of the world's population was Muslim, with Christians comprising nearly 27 percent.[1]

In summary, Islam is growing more quickly in the Western world today than at any other time in history for three main reasons: 1) Muslims are simply having more children than both Christian and non-Christian Westerners; 2) liberal immigration laws have allowed for rapidly-growing Muslim populations throughout the West (particularly in the Netherlands, France, and Germany, countries where the Muslim community is already a significant voice in public affairs); and 3) Muslim proselytism results in many conversions.

As much as the simplicity of Islam is attractive to people, one of the main reasons for conversions among Westerners from Christianity to Islam is dissatisfaction with Christian religious figures and what seems to be an endless wave of scandals. Moreover, the decay of Western culture is seen from the Muslim perspective as a failure of Christianity to provide adequate grounding for society. The human heart hungers for truth, and it is left unsatisfied by the prevailing relativism and lack of moral standards of Western secular culture. All too many Christian denominations, meanwhile, seem more concerned about preaching the latest politically-correct notions rather than the unchanging truths of Christian tradition. While this might attract people in the short run, ultimately it is a hollow exercise that eviscerates a Christian institution's very reason for being — namely, preaching the truths of the Gospel. This sad reality gives proselytizing Muslims a chance to fill the vacuum.

Also, in an information age such as ours, a religion that confidently teaches simple and clear beliefs (such as Islam) is going to have the competitive edge over religions that timidly present vague or "relevant" assertions with little substance.

3. But why does this recent growth of Islam really matter? Why should Catholics care about this?

It is important to keep in mind the radically different kind of world that the rapid rise of Islam portends for our children and grandchildren, a world where the dominance of Islam may erode many of the civil and human rights we now take for granted. Remember — Islam is not merely a religion; it is a social and political ideology that makes sharp distinctions between Muslims and non-Muslims, particularly regarding rights and status. Islam needs to be taken seriously by all, especially by those who profess the "one, holy, catholic, and apostolic" Faith.

It is true that many Catholics remain unconcerned by Islam's rapid growth. There are two possible reasons for this lack of concern: 1) Some Catholics do not understand the theological, spiritual, and cultural ramifications of a world embracing Islam; and 2) Many Catholics suffer from a certain ecclesial complacency based on a misunderstanding of the words of Jesus. After all, Jesus promised that the "gates of hell" would not prevail against His Church (see Mt 16:18). In these words, He promised that the Church would be indestructible and that it would exist throughout the world until the end of time. But Jesus did not promise that Christianity would remain the dominant religion in any particular nation or region (including the United States). Nor did He promise that other religions or creeds — belief systems that do not express as much of the truth about God and man — would not supplant the true Faith in the hearts of many people, even those we love. Above all, He never told us that we would not have to work hard to make sure that the "gates of hell" would not prevail against the Church in our own society. He never promised that His protection of

the Church would be automatic or distinct from the sweat
(and the blood) of His faithful.

4. What is the difference between the terms "Muslim" and "Islam"?

Islam is the name of the religion itself. It means, in Arabic,
"submission to the will of Allah." *Muslim* is a related word
that can be roughly translated as "one who submits" to Allah
and his will. A Muslim, then, is someone who believes in
Islam.[2]

5. I have heard that "Islam" means peace. Is this true?

Since the September 11, 2001 terrorist attacks, many people (including President George W. Bush) have asserted that
Islam means "peace." While it is true that *salaam* (peace) and
Islam (submission) share the same Arabic root, the two words
are by no means synonymous. The word *Muslim* means
"one who submits [that is, surrenders himself] to the will of
Allah." But its broader meaning extends to any person of
any faith who surrenders himself to God's will. This use is
similar to the Christian's use of the term *believer*. However,
Muslims most often use it to refer to someone who believes
in the religion of Islam.

Muslims also use another word to refer to a believer in
Islam: *Mu'men,* which literally means "believer." Westerners
may have heard this term in reference to Afghanistan's Mullah Omar, leader of the Taliban, who proclaimed himself
Emir al Mu'menin (Prince [or Leader] of the Believers). The
two terms *Muslim* and *Mu'men* are used interchangeably in
Arabic, and there is no clear distinction between them.

Whatever terms are used, a Muslim is one who strives to bring his life into line with the will of the one Muslims recognize as the only true God: Allah.

6. What does the Islamic word for God, "Allah", actually mean?

Muslims believe that the true meaning of the word *Allah* is beyond human comprehension and understanding. However, this claim is not supported either by the Koran or Muhammad's Tradition (the *Hadith*). Literally, the word is Arabic for "the God." Some Western scholars of Islamic theology believe this word is of Aramaic origin, while others say it is derived from the Hebrew word *Elohim* — the plural of *El*, the word for God used often in the Old Testament. In any case, Muslims claim that when they call upon Allah they are worshiping the same God that Jews and Christians worship.

From a Catholic perspective, though, Allah (as He is presented in the Koran) is significantly different from the God of Christianity. In the New Testament, Jesus reveals God as a loving Father, a concept utterly foreign (even blasphemous) to a Muslim. For Islam, Allah is only Master, not Father; He demands obedience, not a relationship.

Moreover, in the Old Testament, God reveals Himself as "abounding in steadfast love and faithfulness" (Ex 34:6). The people of Israel saw God's love for them as the reason He chose them from among all peoples and nations to reveal Himself. Speaking through the prophet Jeremiah, God tells His people, "I have loved you with an everlasting love; therefore I have continued my faithfulness to you" (Jer 31:3). God loves His people and asks for their love and faithfulness in return.

7. What is the Koran?

The Koran (sometimes spelled *Qur'an* in English) is the holy book of all Muslims. The word *Koran* means "recital" in Arabic. The Muslim holy book is also called *Al-Furqan* ("The Criterion" or "Standard") and *Al-Mushaf Al-Shreef* ("The Glorious Book") in Arabic.

The Koran as we have it today is comprised of 114 chapters, which are often referred to in English by their Arabic designation, *sura*. Each verse is called *ayat*, which means "sign" or "miracle." This designation came about from Muhammad's reply to those who challenged his claim to be a prophet and asked him to perform a miracle. He claimed that the Koran, and nothing else, was his miracle.

Muslims also often refer to the various suras of the Koran by their titles. These titles are generally derived not so much from the overall subject matter of the chapter, which can be quite wide-ranging, but to one element mentioned in the chapter. For example: Sura 2 is titled "The Cow"; Sura 8, "The Spoils of War"; and Sura 29, "The Spider."

Unlike the Bible, the Koran is not arranged chronologically or by subject matter. Instead, it is arranged according to the length of its chapters. The longest chapter appears first and the shortest chapter last. This organization was completed long after Muhammad's death.

8. Is it true that only the Arabic version of the Koran is considered authentic?

Yes. The Koran is an Arabic book; its Arabic character is part of its essence. Translations of the Koran occupy a curious position in the Islamic world — Muslims do not consider the Koran in any language other than Arabic to be the Koran, since the Arabic version is said to be the word for word revelation of Allah. They claim that Allah spoke to Muhammad in Arabic. This notion comes from the book itself: "We have revealed the Koran in the Arabic tongue so that you may grow in understanding" (Sura 12:1). Translating the Koran into other languages is, however, tolerated for the sake of evangelizing the non-Arab world. Yet in dialogue with non-Arabic speakers, Muslim scholars and apologists often dodge tough questions by dismissing all translations of the Koran and claiming that the book cannot be truly understood in any language other than Arabic. If you do not know Arabic, they maintain, you cannot truly understand the Koran (and, for that matter, Muhammad's Tradition — *the Hadith*).

This entangles Muslims in an inconsistency, since Muslim groups worldwide have undertaken strenuous efforts to convert non-Muslims. These efforts involve translations of the Koran and other Muslim material — translations made by Muslims themselves, despite the alleged impossibility of understanding Islam except in Arabic.[3]

All Muslims, Arab and non-Arab alike, are obligated to pray in Arabic even if they do not understand a single word of what they are reciting or saying. Since today most Muslims are not Arabs, this means that the majority of the world's Muslims recite their Koranic prayers from rote memory. Furthermore, if a Muslim wants to read the Koran, he must read it in Arabic in order to obtain any graces from Allah, even if he does not understand what he is praying.

Although most of the major Islamic commentators on the Koran were not themselves Arabs, nearly all agreed that learning Arabic is mandatory for any Muslim who takes his faith seriously. Ibn Taymiyyah, one of the most influential thinkers in Islamic history and an enduring paragon of Islamic orthodoxy, says:

The Arabic language itself is part of Islam, and knowing Arabic is an obligatory duty. If it is a duty to understand the Qur'an and Sunnah [Muhammad's Tradition], and they cannot be understood without knowing Arabic, then the means that is needed to fulfill the duty is also obligatory.[4]

The religious superiority of Arabic in Islam has led to an Arabic cultural hegemony in the non-Arabic Muslim world. Great non-Arab civilizations in lands that are now Muslim — the most notable example is Iran — are not valued as part of the heritage of the Muslims in those lands, but are generally dismissed as products of the worthless "pre-Islamic time of ignorance."

This is in sharp contrast to the Catholic faith, which is not tied to any particular language or culture and spans the globe without exalting one people at the expense of all others. Truly, the Church of Christ is *catholic* (that is, universal) — it exists everywhere and imposes no particular "culture" of its own. A Catholic believes that the Church's openness to various cultures is the most efficacious (even logical) approach to preaching the Gospel. This is primarily because cultures are temporal creations (that is, they are human in origin and develop over time), while divine truth is eternal — it is not and cannot be bound by any particular culture, race, or language.

9. What are the basic beliefs or tenets of Islam?

In sharp contrast to the multifaceted complexity of Christian theology, Islam is a religion of simplicity. Its primary beliefs are summed up in the *Shahada*, or Confession of Faith: "There is no god but Allah, and Muhammad is His prophet."

When trying to win converts among Christians, Muslims frequently make use of this simplicity as a key selling point.

They compare the length of the Nicene Creed to the brevity of the Shahada and point to the Trinity as a sign that Christianity is not only hopelessly complicated, but illogical — a sharp contrast to Islam's noble simplicity. Former pop singer Cat Stevens, a convert to Islam who now uses the Muslim name Yusuf Islam, recounts his childhood understanding of Christianity this way: "And when they said that God is three, I was puzzled even more but could not argue. I more or less believed it, because I had to have respect for the faith of my parents."[5]

Of course, there is no compelling reason why the truth should be simpler than error. In fact, it is often the other way around, as men unwisely try to tame divine truths by simplifying them.[6] We need to remember that God is radically transcendent and omniscient — that is, He exists eternally distinct from His creation and knows everything as eternally present. He remains, then, an inexhaustible mystery to man, His finite creature. Indeed, He is *the* Mystery. Thus, it should not be surprising if His revelation to us is full of profound mysteries. In any case, Islam's simple faith is summed up in the Shahada, which is the first of the famous Five Pillars of Islam.

10. What are the Five Pillars of Islam?

The Pillars of Islam sum up these central practices of Islam; they are the five most important elements of the Islamic faith. They are: the Confession of Faith (*Shahada*); Prayer (*Salat*); Fasting (*Sawm*); Pilgrimage (*Hajj*); and Almsgiving (*Zakat*).

In contrast to Christianity, Islam is characterized more by practices than by beliefs. In this regard, Islam more closely resembles Judaism than it does Christianity. Christians have historically placed great emphasis on *orthodoxy*, or right belief, whereas Muslims are generally more concerned with *orthopraxy,* the unity of religious practice.

11. What does the first pillar, the Confession of Faith, entail?

The first pillar, as we have seen, is the confession of faith in the unity of Allah and the prophetic status of Muhammad. It is a statement of belief that is also a practice: one becomes a Muslim by making this confession in a public assembly of Muslims. In Arabic this confession is known as the Shahada. Every Muslim must confess verbally and believe that "There is no god but Allah, and Muhammad is His prophet."

To confess this is to become a Muslim, just as baptism makes one a Christian. In form, however, it involves only words, not actions, and it therefore resembles baptism less than it does the confession of Jesus Christ as personal Savior that makes one a Christian according to many in the evangelical Protestant tradition.

According to Islamic theology, the first part of this testimony, "There is no god but Allah," consists of three elements:

1. *The oneness of Allah*: although He refers to Himself in the Koran using the first-person plural reserved to kings ("We"), He is an absolute unity.

2. *The confession that Allah is the only One that human beings should worship.* This was formulated as a rejection of the Christian doctrine of the Trinity.

3. *The confession of His Holy Names (of which there are 99) and Essence,* here subsumed under the name Allah.

The second part of the Shahada contains the assertion that Muhammad is Allah's prophet. Implied is the assertion that all humans are obligated to follow Him as the final prophet of Allah and the perfect example for all humanity to imitate.

12. Muslims seem to be very dedicated to prayer.

Yes, they are. The second pillar of Islam is prayer (*Salat*). Prayers are mandatory five times a day for all Muslims. Muslims generally regard this as the greatest pillar of the faith, the unbendable pillar. Muslims may be excused from observing the other pillars — fasting, almsgiving, pilgrimage to Mecca — when their health, age, finances, or some other impediment do not permit them to perform these duties. But never is anyone formally excused from praying five times a day.

Part of the Muslim's prayer obligation is attendance at community prayers in the local mosque on Fridays. Most Muslims regard attending these community prayers as essential to their practice of the faith, because there is strength in unity and praying together.

The daily call to prayer is called *Athan*. In Muslim countries nowadays it is announced through loudspeakers. The person who calls the faithful to prayer by chanting the Athan is called a *Mu'athin* (or *Muezzin*). A Mu'athin calls the Athan five times a day, just before the times when Muslims are required to perform their daily prayers. The Athan is composed of specific words and phrases that the Mu'athin must recite loudly, beginning with *Allahu Akbar* ("Allah is great").

Before a Muslim can pray, he ordinarily must perform a series of ritual ablutions (*Wudu*). He must wash each fist, his hands to the elbow, his face, ears, nose, and feet three times, as well as his sexual organs. There are also a number of bowings and prostrations (*Rukha*) that are part of each prayer. They consist of many movements, each of which is accompanied by a recitation of certain prayers.

The daily prayers are said in the early morning, at noon, at mid-afternoon, at sunset, and at night.[7] Muslims often criticize Christians for failing to pray as faithfully as Muslims do. Indeed, with some notable exceptions (particularly the *hesychasm* of Eastern Christianity), Muslims could well be correct in this criticism. Too few Christians have embodied St. Paul's command to "pray without ceasing" (1 Thess 5:17).[8]

The Koran mentions three times daily when prayers should be said (see Sura 11:114). According to Muhammad's Tradition, the Prophet received the command to pray five times a day from Allah himself, during the Prophet's mystical Night Journey to Heaven. Muhammad says that he was originally told by Allah to command his followers to pray *fifty* times daily, but Allah later revealed this to be too much of a burden.[9]

13. Why do Muslims worship on Friday? Isn't Sunday the Lord's Day?

Christians gather to observe the Sabbath on Sunday because that is the day the Lord Jesus rose from the dead. Muslims, however, deny the resurrection of Christ. They gather on Friday according to the command of the Koran, which seems to have been laid down in order to distinguish Muslims from Jews (who gather on Saturdays) and Christians: "O ye who believe! When the call is proclaimed to prayer on Friday (the Day of Assembly), hasten earnestly to the Remembrance of Allah, and leave off business (and traffic): That is best for you if ye but knew!" (Sura 62:9)

14. Are mosques considered churches? Do Muslims have to go to a mosque to pray?

The answer to both questions is no. Mosques have traditionally been the center of the Muslim community, and accordingly have been focal points of artistic expression in the Islamic world. Muslims are encouraged to pray in mosques because graces are multiplied in community prayer. Mosque attendance is mandatory, however, on Fridays and Feast Days, as well as for funerals.

Some of the world's greatest architectural wonders are mosques, including the al-Aqsa mosque and the Dome of the Rock in Jerusalem, and the Aya Sofya mosque in Istanbul. The two Jerusalem mosques were built according to the model of Byzantine churches. The Aya Sofya is itself a former Byzantine church: the Hagia Sophia, the jewel of Christendom for a thousand years prior to the Muslim conquest of Constantinople in 1453. Al-Aqsa and the Dome of the Rock were constructed in the seventh century after Muslim armies took Jerusalem. Both, of course, have become symbols of the religious and cultural tensions of Jerusalem, and this is nothing new: the Dome of the Rock was purposely constructed on the site of the old Jewish Temple in the same spirit with which Muslims bricked up the Jerusalem gate through which the Messiah was expected to enter.

15. What are Islam's rules regarding fasting?

Fasting is the third pillar of Islam. Every Muslim is obligated to fast during the ninth month of the Islamic calendar, *Ramadan*, which literally means "parched thirst." According to the prophet Muhammad, "Verily, the smell of the mouth of a fasting person is better to Allah than the smell of musk."[10]

Because Islam follows a lunar calendar, the month of Ramadan slowly travels through the year; in some years it falls in the hottest part of summer, and in other years in the most frigid times of winter. During Ramadan, Muslims must abstain from all eating, drinking, smoking, and sexual relations from just before sunrise until sunset.

Muslims consider the month of Ramadan holy because they believe it was during this month Muhammad received the initial revelation of the Koran. Also in this same month, Muhammad is believed to have ascended to the Seven Heavens upon his death. At first, the fast lasted only three days, but over time it became extended to an entire month.

16. Why are Muslims required to make a pilgrimage to Mecca?

At least once during their lifetimes, Muslims are obligated to make a pilgrimage (*Hajj*) to the holiest site in Islam: the city of Mecca in Saudi Arabia, where Muhammad was born and where he lived for a great part of his tumultuous life.[11] The hajj is the fourth pillar of Islam. If the Muslim is physically and financially able to undertake this pilgrimage, he must do so. If not, he is exempted from this obligation.

Muslims cannot make this pilgrimage any time they choose: the *hajj* takes place only during the twelfth month in the lunar calendar, Dhu al-Hijjah.

The Muslim pilgrim (*Hajji*) must fulfill two conditions; otherwise, his hajj is unacceptable. First, he must have a right intention to worship Allah alone, along with a desire for the Hereafter. Also, he must follow the example of Muhammad in words and deeds, performing the specific rituals as Muhammad did in his life. If the pilgrim performs these rituals improperly, or makes the journey because of a desire to be seen by men, or for any other worldly reason, his pilgrimage is worthless.

The pilgrimage involves a number of ritual actions. The pilgrims visit several important sites, including the well of Zamzam, where the angel Gabriel is said to have slaked the thirst of Hagar and Ishmael. At a certain point the pilgrims throw rocks at Satan, just as Abraham is supposed to have done at the same site when the Evil One tempted him. At another place the pilgrims sacrifice an animal.

The focal point of the pilgrimage, however, is the small stone building known as the *Ka'aba* (cube). Many Muslims consider it to be the very house of Allah on earth. It is a bare room with stone walls, and can accommodate about fifty people. It contains the black stone, which Allah is said to have thrown down from Heaven. Hajjis kiss it reverently. The Ka'aba was a pagan shrine before the advent of Islam, although Islamic tradition holds that the angel Gabriel gave Abraham the black stone and that he constructed a shrine there. In pre-Islamic times, the room that contains the black stone was the place where the local pagans kept statues of their gods. According to some Muslim traditions, there were even images of Mary and Jesus there.

Although many Muslims believe that Abraham built the Ka'aba, the Koran states that it was built before Abraham. In Sura 2:127 Abraham seems to be the builder of the House — that is, the Ka'aba. Sura 14:37, however, speaks of Abraham placing Ishmael and Hagar by the sacred house, which means that it already existed. Adam himself is said to have built the first shrine on the spot. Ishmael and Muhammad are supposed to have built and rebuilt there, too.

It seems more likely that Muhammad was able to win over some converts to his new faith, and to avoid alienating others, by incorporating certain rituals from the pagan Ka'aba into Islam.

17. What does Islam teach about almsgiving?

Muslims believe that almsgiving (*zakat*) purifies the property of the giver and purifies his heart from selfishness and greed. The Muslim view here closely coincides with the Christian idea of charity: almsgiving provides the poor with sustenance and minimizes jealousy and envy. It restores the right balance between the giver and the receiver. Thus, almsgiving is Islam's fifth and final pillar.

In many Muslim countries the zakat is collected much as a tax would be. Muslim jurists differ on how much a Muslim should pay, but most agree that the zakat should not be less than 2.5 percent of a Muslim's net property, after he has paid all expenses required by the law and the faith. In some Islamic countries, the mosques have the responsibility to distribute the money to the poor and needy.

The Five Pillars are generally all that non-Muslims know about Islamic beliefs and practices, but Muslims also hold Six Articles of faith.

18. What are the Six Articles of the Islamic faith?

Throughout its history, Islam has seen much less dogmatic elaboration than has Christianity, but it is not altogether free of such concerns. There is not wide latitude in what Muslims may believe, and although there is a multiplicity of sects (such as Sunni and Shi'ite) within Islam, there is broad unanimity about the central elements of the faith and how it must be practiced.

The Six Articles of Faith are mandatory for anyone who calls himself a Muslim. They are:

1. Belief in Allah and His unity

This is the first and most important article in Islam. The most important elements of this declaration are: 1) Allah is not united with other deities, and no others are consubstantial with or equal to Him in any way; 2) He has no partners (that is, wives) and no son, and He has no need of a son. The Koran, as we shall see, considers the idea of God's having a son to be an offense against His transcendent majesty; and 3) His nature cannot be comprehended, and He does not reveal it — except to insist that He does not and cannot have a Son.[12]

2. Belief in Allah's prophets

The Koran mentions twenty-five prophets by name, eighteen of whom are mentioned in the Old Testament. Three others — Zechariah, John the Baptist, and Jesus Christ — appear in the New Testament, and the other four are found in Arabian sources. The Koran states that all of these prophets were given revelations identical to those found in the Koran.

The Koran also places Muhammad firmly within the line of Jewish biblical prophets, even though Muhammad was not a Jew (Sura 3:84). Muhammad claimed to be from the line of Ishmael, thus establishing a connection between himself and Abraham. It has been common to the present day for Islam and Arabs to be identified with Ishmael, although not all Arabs claim that they are from the line of Ishmael. A Catholic would point out, however, that aside from a few sketchy accounts of non-biblical prophets, there is no trace in the Koran of a prophetic line outside the biblical one. Still, Muslims believe that Allah has also sent prophets for all nations of the earth (see Sura 16:36).[13] They believe that the differences we see today between Judaism, Christianity, and Islam exist because Jews and Christians were not faithful to Allah's true message.

3. Belief in Allah's revelations

Muslims must believe in the revelations that were given to these prophets who were sent to every nation. But there is no content to this belief beyond believing in the Koran. Muslims believe not only that the names of most of the prophets sent around the world have vanished from memory, but also that their "books" have all perished. Outside of the pure and perfect Koran, only the Bible survives, but Muslims believe (as we shall discuss in a later question) that today's Bible contains only corrupted versions of the original revelations.

4. Belief in Allah's angels

It may seem strange that a religion as stridently monotheistic as Islam would include belief in angels as part of its core beliefs. There are many reasons why this is so — notably the Koran's mysterious and fascinating teachings about the angel Gabriel, whom Muslims believe delivered Allah's revelation of the Koran to Muhammad.[14]

Muslims agree with Christians and Jews that angels, like humans, are creatures of Allah (see Sura 35:1). No one can win favor in Allah's sight who rejects the angels: "Whoever is an enemy to Allah and His angels and messengers, to Gabriel and Michael, Lo! Allah is their enemy to those who reject Faith" (Sura 2:98).[15]

5. Belief in Fate

The absence of a firm belief in causality (that is, that all realities and occurrences have a discernable cause or origin in something else) in Islam is a reflection of the pre-Islamic concept of fate or destiny, *Qadar*. This concept is evident throughout the Koran. In the Koran, everyone's destiny or fate is in the hands of Allah: "Say: 'Nothing shall ever happen to us except what Allah has ordained for us. He is our *Maula* (Lord, Helper, and Protector).' And in Allah let the believers put their trust" (Sura 9:51; see also Sura 64:11).

Allah's providential care is absolute, even for spiritual good and ill. One Hadith (that is, Tradition of Muhammad) has Adam besting Moses, who is scolding him for his sin, by appealing to the fact that Allah controls everything that happens: "Allah's Apostle said, 'Adam and Moses argued with each other. Moses said to Adam. "You are Adam whose mistake expelled you from Paradise." Adam said to him, "You are Moses whom Allah selected as His Messenger and as the one to whom He spoke directly; yet you blame me for a thing which had already been written in my fate before my creation?"' Allah's Apostle said twice, 'So, Adam overpowered Moses.'"[16] The Hadith (plural: *Ahadith*) is second in authority only to the Koran for most Muslims.

Catholic theology would contend that the concept of fate is extremely damaging to true religious faith. If all things are arbitrarily determined by God, then human free will is crippled, and human responsibility therefore becomes nonexistent. From a Catholic perspective, deterministic fate is contrary to the God of the Bible, a God who desires that we freely love Him and freely choose His will for our lives. God's providential care of the world He created always respects human freedom; He never forces us to do anything. We are *not* puppets on the string of a divine puppet master; we are, rather, free sons and daughters of a loving God.

6. Belief in Judgment Day

The Day of Judgment looms large especially in the apocalyptic early suras of the Koran, which contain arresting poetic warnings of the divine wrath to come (see Sura 82:1–19).

The Koran is also quite explicit in describing the joys awaiting believers and the horrors in store for unbelievers after the dreadful Day. It presents both joys and horrors in completely physical terms: Heaven, as we shall see in question 70, is full of the pleasures of the flesh, while Hell is a horrific torture chamber (see Sura 4:56).

As we have seen, people enter Heaven or Hell solely according to the will of Allah. However, the Koran also quite often presents Heaven as the reward of faith and good deeds: "But those who have faith and work righteousness, they are companions of the Garden: Therein shall they abide [forever]" (Sura 2:82; see also Sura 2:257).

Among the signs of Judgment Day, Islamic tradition holds that the greatest of all is the second coming of Jesus Christ! It is He, not Muhammad or anyone else, whom Muslims expect to return to earth in the last days. Why Jesus will return, and not Muhammad, is not clearly explained in Muhammad's Tradition. This is likely another example of Christian theology acting as the source of Muhammad's esoteric doctrine.

In Catholic belief, Christ's Second Coming in glory is necessarily linked to His first coming in the Incarnation: it is the necessary conclusion of His saving mission. Jesus returns at the end of time to judge all mankind and so bring the history of salvation to a close.

19. I have heard that Muslims sometimes call the angel Gabriel the "Holy Spirit." Do they mean this the same way Christians do?

Although Gabriel is the "Holy Spirit" and sometimes simply "the Spirit" (Sura 97:4), Muslims consider him to be only a creature of Allah. The words *Holy Spirit* do not have the connotation of divinity for Muslims that they do for Christians. For a Christian, the Holy Spirit is the third Person of the Trinity; the Spirit shares in the divine nature with God the Father and the Son.

Calling the angel Gabriel "Spirit" and "Holy Spirit" without qualification thus entangles Muslims in some difficulty. If he is simply "the Spirit," does the Koran mean to say that he is the Spirit of Allah? And if so, wouldn't that make him an eternal, uncreated being, since the eternal God could never have existed without His Spirit? To escape this conclusion, Muslims would have to differentiate various aspects of Allah's Nature, but to do so would compromise their monotheism.

Of course, the Koranic record is not clear about Gabriel: it does not say explicitly that he is the Spirit of Allah, but it comes close enough to raise uncomfortable questions for Muslims. When Gabriel appeared to Mary and the "spirit entered in her" or, as it says in Sura 66:12: "we breathed in her Our spirit" it is evident that the spirit meant is the Spirit of Allah. The great Muslim commentator on the Koran, Ibn Kathir, has this comment on Sura 66:12: "*we breathed in her*, through the angel Gabriel, whom God sent and who resembled to Mary as a full man and God commanded him to breathe in her — and this breath dwelt in her womb and became Jesus [emphasis added]."[17]

Again, it is highly likely that these problems arise because fragments of Christian theology have been imported, with some adulterations, more or less wholesale into the Koran.

20. Where was Islam founded and by whom?

According to Islamic tradition, the prophet Muhammad (A.D. 570–632) began receiving revelations (*Wahy*) from Allah through the angel Gabriel in the city of Mecca, in what is now Saudi Arabia, in the year 610. Muhammad was born in Arabia and spent the first forty years of his life as a merchant. These revelations continued until his death on June 8, 632.

Although Muhammad introduced teachings that had never before been part of Jewish or Christian tradition, Muslims believe that Islam is the natural and original religion of all human beings, and that it was preached by the prophets of Judaism and Christianity. As such, Muslims do not generally regard Muhammad as the founder of Islam, but merely as its final prophet.[18]

Muhammad believed that his revelations were in some kind of continuity with Judaism and Christianity. Therefore, Muslims would say the founder of Islam is Allah himself in his revelations to all the prophets.

21. According to Muslim belief, how did Muhammad receive Allah's revelations?

According to his favorite wife, Aisha, Muhammad was chosen as a prophet after devoting himself to prayer for long periods. He received his revelations in dreams after long periods of seclusion in the cave of Hira. It is said that the Truth came to him in the form of the angel Gabriel.

This is the famous first revelation of the Koran, now found as Sura 96:1–5.[19] It began a series of messages from Allah that would continue off and on for the rest of Muhammad's life. Muhammad seems to have gone into a trance-like state to receive them, and he would recite them when he returned to consciousness. His followers committed his messages to memory and wrote them on whatever was available, and as we have seen, they were collected into the Koran after his death.

At the beginning, however, Muhammad was not at all sure what was happening to him. He returned to his wife Khadija from his first meeting with Gabriel in a state of tremendous distress: "Then Allah's Messenger returned with the Revelation, and with his heart beating severely till he entered upon Khadija and said, 'Cover me! Cover me!' They covered him till his fear was over and then he said, 'O Khadija, what is wrong with me?' Then he told her everything that had happened and said, 'I fear that something may happen to me.' "[20]

Khadija, according to this Hadith, had more confidence in Muhammad than he did in himself. She responded, "Never! By Allah! But have the glad tidings, for by Allah, Allah will never disgrace you as you keep good relations with your kith and kin, speak the truth, help the poor and the destitute, serve your guests generously and assist the deserving, calamity-afflicted ones."[21]

Khadija and Muhammad then went to visit her cousin Waraqa,[22] a Christian, who could write in Hebrew and had knowledge of the Gospels. Waraqa confirmed that Muhammad's revelations were genuine and warned Muhammad that he would face hostility and opposition for making them known.[23]

Without Khadija's care and Waraqa's affirmation, the world might never have known Islam, for the new prophet's distress and uncertainty were intense. Soon after Waraqa identified the being who had appeared to Muhammad, Waraqa died, Allah's revelations ceased, and the new prophet was plunged into a sadness so intense that he even contemplated suicide by throwing himself off of a mountain. Every time he went up the top of the mountain, however, the angel Gabriel would appear and give him assurances that he was indeed Allah's messenger, and his peace would be restored.

Muslims throughout history have been embarrassed by the

fact that Muhammad's prophetic mission was confirmed in its earliest stages by a Christian (who was also a priest and a convert from Judaism). Some Muslim sources deny that Waraqa was a Christian at all, but this fact is well-attested not only in the Hadith but also by a ninth-century biographer of Muhammad, Ibn Hisham: "It has been said about the priest Waraqa that, he was of the religion of Moses, then of the religion of Esa [Jesus], may peace be upon them."[24]

22. Did Muhammad claim to be divine?

No. Muhammad claimed to be a messenger from Allah and a warner of His impending punishment of unbelievers (Sura 7:188). He emphatically insisted that he was only a human being, and not in any way divine. In the Koran, Allah directs him: "Say: 'I am but a man like yourselves, but the inspiration has come to me that your God is one God'" (Sura 18:110).

23. Is it true that Muhammad was an army leader or general?

Yes. Muhammad was a political and military leader as well as a preacher of his word. It was common among religious leaders of his day to have both prophetic and military roles. Muhammad led thirty-two raids and fought three major wars.

In fact, Islam begins its calendar not from the date of Muhammad's first revelation, nor from his birth. Instead, it begins with the date of Muhammad's flight from Mecca to Medina (the *hegira*), when he became the head of a community and an army for the first time. In 624, he began a series of raids on the surrounding tribes, and defeated a large force from his own tribe, the *Quraysh*, at Mecca. Other victorious battles followed. By 628 Muhammad had reached an accord with the Quraysh and returned to Mecca, where he smashed all the pagan idols in the Ka'aba. (According to legend, he ordered an icon of Jesus and His Mother to remain untouched.)

As may be expected of a seventh-century military leader, he could be harsh and unforgiving. When his uncle Abu Lahab publicly rejected his prophetic message, he cursed him and his wife in words that have become an entire sura of the Koran: "May the hands of Abu Lahab perish! May he himself perish! Nothing shall his wealth and gains avail him. He shall be burnt in a flaming fire, and his wife, laden with faggots, shall have a rope of fibre around her neck!" (Sura 111:1–5). This is an important element of the example that Muhammad has given to the Muslim world.

24. I have heard about Shiite and Sunni Muslims. What are the main differences between these groups?

There are several key groups in Islam today. Three of the largest and most well-known are:

1. Sunnis. These comprise around 85 percent of Muslims worldwide. The word *Sunni* is related to *Sunna*, or "tradition." Sunni Muslims follow doctrines and practices derived from the Sunna of the Prophet — that is, the Traditions (*Hadith*) as interpreted by Muslim scholars throughout history.

The *Wahhabis,* who are prevalent in Saudi Arabia, are a Sunni subsect. Muhammad ibn Abd al-Wahhab (1703–1792) was a reformer. He wanted to rid Islam of everything that had developed after the first few centuries. He stressed a literal reading of the Koran and Hadith that made the Wahhabis a furious, violent sect that even made war against other Muslim groups it considered heretical. The Wahhabis control Saudi Arabia today, and from there aggressively export Wahhabism around the world. Some of the terrorists involved in the September 11, 2001 attacks were members of this group.

2. *Shi'ites.* The word *Shi'a* is short for *Shi'at Ali*, or "the party of Ali." This is the largest non-Sunni sect. Shi'ite Muslims believe that Ali, the husband of Muhammad's daughter Fatima, was the Prophet's only rightful successor as leader of the Muslim community. Shi'ites have traditions and practices that are quite distinct from those of the Sunnis. Notable among these is the belief that the *Imams* (that is, leaders) who succeeded Ali in Muhammad's prophetic line inherited Muhammad's prophetic spirit. Most Shi'ites believe that there were twelve such Imams, and that the last one disappeared from the earth and will return as the Mahdi, a Messianic figure, at the end of the age.

3. *Sufis.* The Sufis are the mystical sect in Islam, although Shi'ite Islam also bears strong marks of mystical influence. The Sufis stress love for Allah and union with him in terms that often strongly resemble Christian mysticism. They have been and still are ferociously persecuted as heretics in many areas of the Islamic world.

Other notable sects include the Baha'is of Iran (who have a presence in the United States as well), the Kharijites of Oman, and the Alawites of Syria. These are often considered heretics by the larger Muslim groups.

Regarding the Sunnis and Shi'ites, there are many differences in emphasis and style of spiritual expression, but the chief differences are the Sunni emphasis on the Prophet's Sunna (traditions) as the guide for believers, and the Shi'ite belief in the Imam as the inheritor of the "light of Muhammad" and leader of the Muslim community. The Imams were the infallible interpreters of Islamic tradition. Many Shi'ites believe that their infallibility passes to their regents as the leaders of the Muslims, such as Iran's Ayatollah Khomeini.

Shi'ites do not accept the legitimacy of the first three Caliphs who succeeded Muhammad. They differ with Sunnis over the legitimacy of temporary marriage (Shi'ites accept it, Sunnis do not), the conduct of prayers, and the doctrine of the *Mahdi*, or the hidden Imam, who will come on Judgment Day to restore peace and justice on earth.

Shi'ite spirituality is likewise more mystical than that of the Sunnis, with intense veneration of Ali, prayers at the tombs of prophets and Muslim saints, and a strong focus on suffering and martyrdom.

25. Were there Jews and Christians living in Arabia before Islam?

Though most of the tribes in the Arabia of Muhammad's time were pagan and polytheistic, there were large communities of Christians in both Arabia and Yemen. Few of these Christian communities, however, were orthodox; most advocated one or more of the heresies of the time, including Arianism, Monophysitism, and Nestorianism. All of these heresies held false or incomplete views of the nature of Christ. Muhammad's exposure to Christianity, therefore, seems to have been limited to contact with heretical Christian groups. As a result, he seems never to have gained a clear, orthodox understanding of the Gospel. Moreover, Christianity's penetration into the Arabian peninsula at this point was slight and haphazard, and there were few that called themselves Christians who could clearly and accurately explain what they believed.

As noted above (and as the Koran affirms), these heretical groups hotly disputed the nature of Christ. The Arians taught that Jesus was a created being; the Monophysites claimed that His humanity was subsumed into His divinity; and the Nestorians upheld both His humanity and His divinity, but with a sharp distinction between the two. (In fact, Khadija's cousin, Waraqa, is sometimes identified as a Nestorian.) The Nestorians also denied the title of "Mother of God" to Mary, as she was, they insisted, the mother of Jesus' human nature only. These ideas could very well have been the basis for Muhammad's mistaken belief that the Trinity consisted of Allah, Mary, and Jesus.

The Koran also denies the crucifixion of Christ — it claims that Jesus only *seemed* to be crucified (see Sura 4:157). This may point to a Gnostic influence, since Gnostic Christians also taught that someone else was made to look like Jesus and put on the Cross. There were also some Manicheans in Arabia at this time, and they too became imbued with many of these false notions about the crucifixion.[25]

26. What are the reasons Jews and Muslims cannot seem to get along? Is this rooted in religion, culture, or both?

Both. In Muhammad's day, Jews were concentrated in Medina (then known as Yathrib) and elsewhere along the trade routes in Arabia. There were several powerful Jewish tribes in close proximity to Muhammad in the early days of his prophetic career, and he seems to have assumed that they would accept his monotheistic message and his claim to be a prophet.

The Jews, however, were not at all eager to accept a non-Jew as a prophet. They were powerful in Arabia in those days, and they began to create serious problems for the new prophet. Rejected, Muhammad turned on the Jews fiercely, even referring to them as "apes and swine."[26]

Nor did the Prophet restrict his response to Jewish scorn and disbelief to mere curses. He ordered the assassination of several Jewish leaders and people of influence, including Asma bint Marwan, a woman with small children. Her crime? Writing crude and indecent verses that mocked the Prophet. When news of her murder was brought to Muhammad, he rejoiced.[27]

Throughout history Muslims have criticized Jews for rejecting the Prophet. The enmity between Jews and Muslims is reinforced by a Hadith which says "Abu Huraira reported Allah's Messenger (may peace be upon him) as saying: The last hour would not come unless the Muslims will fight against the Jews and the Muslims would kill them until the Jews would hide themselves behind a stone or a tree and a stone or a tree would say: Muslim, or the servant of Allah, there is a Jew behind me; come and kill him."[28] This tradition is repeated, with small variations, numerous times in the Hadith.

Today there is animosity between Muslims and Jews caused by the conflict between Israelis and Palestinians, but this animosity is intensified by Islamic religious concepts. Some harsh words in the Koran support this animosity. In one notorious verse, Jews are called "sons of pigs and monkeys" (Sura 5:59–60) Muslim radicals routinely make use of this reference, and it is not difficult to see why the two groups have trouble getting along given such disagreeable terms.

27. Why was Muhammad's prophetic claim rejected by the Jews and Christians of his time?

Muhammad's failure to understand the basic beliefs of Judaism and Christianity was a principal reason why both groups of his day did not believe that he was a prophet. Also, it was common for people in the ancient world to ask for a sign, which normally involved miracles, of someone who claimed to be a prophet. The Jews asked Jesus many times to perform miracles to prove He was the Messiah. Elijah and Moses, as well as others who were sent to the people of Israel, performed miracles as testimony that their messages were from God.

Muhammad, however, was unable to present a single miracle to those who rejected him. His failure to present a miracle, and his defensiveness in the face of those who dismissed his prophetic claims as a result, is evident throughout the Koran. Allah supposedly tells Muhammad's followers that "your companion [Muhammad] is not seized with madness: he is but a perspicuous warner" (Sura 7:184); and "your companion is not one possessed" (Sura 85:22). Allah repeatedly reassures Muhammad himself that "you are no soothsayer, nor are you one possessed" (Sura 52:29); and "You are not, by the grace of your Lord, mad or possessed" (Sura 68:2).

As we have seen, Muhammad's own distress and uncertainty when he first began to receive revelations led him to the brink of suicide. Ultimately, however, Muslim tradition began to hold that his message was a miracle in itself, primarily because he himself was illiterate.

28. Was Muhammad really illiterate, as Muslims claim?

Muslims claim that Muhammad was illiterate in order to affirm what they consider to be the miraculous character of the Koran. This sublime book of poetry, they say, could not have been written by any ordinary man — and certainly not by one who was illiterate. However, this claim of Muhammad's illiteracy has no actual Koranic support at all.

Islamic commentators on the Koran and the Hadith base their claims on the Arabic word *ome*, which they translate as "illiterate." This is one meaning of the word, but it has another meaning that has nothing to do with reading or writing. The Koran's use of the word establishes that this secondary meaning is the one it is using. Sura 62:2 says, "It is He that sent forth among the *omeyeen* [the plural of *ome*] an apostle of their own. . . ." This same word is repeated in many other places in the Koran, including Suras 2:78; 3:20; 3:75; and 7:157–158. Almost all Muslim scholars interpret the word *omeyeen* in these passages as meaning "illiterate." Yet if the word *omeyeen* refers to illiteracy, Sura 62:2 would be saying that Allah sent forth to all illiterates one of their own.

In fact, in classical Arabic, *omeyeen* never referred to illiterates or to illiteracy. It refers to non-Jewish people: the verse says that Allah has sent a Gentile apostle to the Gentiles. *Omeyeen* is an adjectival form of the Arabic noun for Gentiles, and not all Gentiles were illiterate during the time of Muhammad.

29. Did Muhammad write the Koran?

No, he did not. But although Muhammad himself did not write any of it, the Koran very much reflects the concerns of the Prophet and his seventh-century community. During his lifetime, his followers recorded his revelations on any material they had handy, but most of all they committed them to memory in what was primarily an oral culture. The collection of all of Muhammad's alleged revelations into one volume only began in earnest when the ongoing holy wars, or *jihads*, being waged by Muslims raised the real possibility that the only person who had committed an important revelation to memory might be killed in battle, and the revelation would be lost forever.

30. How is the Koran different from the Bible?

In content, the closest books to the Koran in the Bible are the five books of Moses — Genesis, Exodus, Leviticus, Numbers, and Deuteronomy. The Muslim holy book has the same mix of laws and narratives about God's dealings with His people. But the Koran is unlike any book of the Bible in that there is only one speaker throughout: Allah (although there are a few exceptions to this that bedevil Muslims to this day).[29]

While the Pentateuch presents a more or less continuous narrative from the creation of the world to the Israelites' imminent entry into the Promised Land, the Koran makes no attempt at linear history. Though the Koran is shorter than the New Testament, a surprisingly large amount of what it says is repeated. Nevertheless, the reader often cannot figure out what exactly is being said, or why, without reference to the Hadith. We will examine this later.

31. Does the Bible play any role in Islamic belief and practice?

Not as such, but the Koran's primary message — namely, that there is one God, Allah, and the worst of all sins is idolatry — has strong biblical parallels. Also, the basic outline of its story will be familiar to Bible readers, although in the Koran the story of salvation is altered in significant ways.

After Adam and Eve were deceived by Satan into turning away from the truth (a story imported straight from Genesis, with important modifications and embellishments), Allah sent the world a succession of prophets to call people back to true worship. The most important of these were Noah, Abraham, Isaac, Jacob and, as one Koranic passage lists them, "David and Solomon, Job and Joseph and Moses and Aaron . . . ; Zacharias and John, Jesus and Elias . . . ; and Ishmael, Elisha, Jonah and Lot" (Sura 6:84–87). As we shall soon see in greater detail, Jesus here is mentioned as a merely human member of this roster of prophets, not as the Son of God.

Along with the biblical prophets, the Koran is full of Bible stories — mainly Old Testament tales along with a few taken from heretical Christian gospels. For example, the twelfth story tells of Joseph and his brothers, although it is shorn of its significance for Israel as a nation; Noah's ark appears in Sura 10; Jonah and his whale appear in Sura 37; and Moses figures prominently throughout the Koran. All this gave rise to charges against Muhammad during his lifetime that he was passing off warmed-over Bible stories as revelations from Allah. This suspicion persists, despite Allah's apparent denials: "But the misbelievers say: 'Naught is this but a lie which he has forged, and others have helped him at it.' In truth it is they who have put forward an iniquity and a falsehood. . . . Say: 'The [Qur'an] was sent down by Him who knows the mystery [that is] in the heavens and the earth: verily He is Oft-Forgiving, Most Merciful' " (Sura 25:4–6).

32. Are there different versions of the Koran?

Muslims strongly deny the existence of any versions of the Koran other than the one they consider to be the one true version in classical Arabic. However, the facts of the case are not quite so simple. Islamic apologists point to the almost complete lack of textual variants in early manuscripts of the Koran as evidence that Allah is, indeed, preserving the book, in contrast to the many variations one finds in biblical manuscripts.

However, this situation is artificial. Muhammad never gathered together all his revelations, which his followers had written not only on paper but on whatever they could find: bark, skin, rock, and bone. After his death in 632, several Muslim communities had their own copies of the Koran, each collected by different followers of Muhammad. But the Caliph Uthman, who ruled Islam from 644 to 656, found himself presiding over a fractious community whose squabbles were fueled by Koranic variants. Consequently, he ordered a single canonical copy of the Koran made and all others destroyed.[30]

Most scholars believe that Uthman's act was the chief agent of the miraculous integrity of the Koranic text.[31] In any case, despite Uthman's best efforts, textual variants continued to exist. One version of the Koran collected by Abdullah ibn Mas'ud, one of Muhammad's servants, contains a number of variant readings and omits three Suras that appear in the canonical text; another version adds two short Suras that are not in the canonical version. Shi'ite Muslims, one of Islam's chief sects, have a version of the Koran with variations from that used by the Sunni.

In 1972, construction workers who were restoring the Great Mosque of Sana'a in Yemen chanced upon a cache of ancient manuscripts. These turned out to be pages of the Koran dating back to the seventh and eighth centuries, many of which contained passages that differed from the canonical and universally accepted Koran. Although most of these differences were minor, their very existence was enormously significant, for they represented a fresh challenge to the Muslim assumption that the Koran is the perfect Word of Allah Himself, sent from Heaven and preserved in pristine form without any variants at all. The original text is preserved in Heaven on golden tablets.

Other scholars have found evidence that challenges the common Islamic claim that the Koran was fully compiled during the reign of Uthman. "There is no hard evidence," says Patricia Crone, author of *Hagarism: The Making of the Islamic World*, "for the existence of the Koran in any form before the last decade of the seventh century."[32] If this is true, of course, it casts doubt upon the accepted Islamic understanding of the prophecy of Muhammad and, indeed, about his status as a true prophet.

33. What does the Koran teach about Jesus?

In the Koran, Jesus is ordinarily called Jesus the Messiah (*Isa Al-Masih*) or Jesus, Son of Mary.

There are several strange aspects of this. The Arabic name used for Jesus in the Koran is *Isa*, which actually corresponds more closely to Esau, the oldest son of Jacob, than it does to Jesus. Also, while Jesus is called the Messiah in the Koran, this word seems to function more like a proper name (*Al-Masih*) than a title. Indeed, no Jewish or Christian understandings of the Messiah as "anointed one" are present in the Koran. The classical Islamic commentators interpret the name *Masih* as a derivation of the Arabic verb *Massaha*, which means to rub, anoint or touch someone for the sake of healing — clearly a derivation of the original Hebrew. But Muslims turn the notion inside out: instead of being the Anointed One of God, they say that Jesus was called *Masih* because He was a healer, that is, He was the one doing the anointing.

The fact that the Koran calls Jesus the Son of Mary emphasizes His virgin birth. No one in those days would have been called the son of anyone but his father — unless his father were unknown.

The Koran agrees with the Bible about the miraculous virgin birth of Jesus. However, it disagrees about the implications of this event. In the Koran, the Virgin Birth does not point to the divinity of Christ; rather, it is only another sign of Allah's supreme power and wisdom. The fact that Jesus was sinless is like saying He had on a nice suit Allah gave Him, but it says nothing about the nature of Jesus Himself (see Suras 19:21 and 23:50).

The Koran also gives other supposed details of Jesus' birth that are not found in the canonical Gospels. As He does in the infancy narratives of the heretical gospels, Jesus in the Koran even speaks in His cradle.[33]

Also, according to the Koran Jesus was not born in a manger, but under a palm tree outside the city. About Mary, the Koran says: "And the pains of childbirth drove her to the trunk of a palm-tree: She cried [in her anguish]: 'Ah! would that I had died before this! Would that I had been a thing forgotten and out of sight!'" (Sura 19:23).

These are a few examples of how Muslims believe that the Koran corrects the biblical account. They are unmoved by Christians arguing that the biblical account is more reliable than that of the Koran because it was written so much closer to the events. Muslims believe the Koran retells biblical accounts precisely to correct them where they have been corrupted by Jews and Christians.

34. Is it true that Muslims consider Jesus a prophet?

Yes. Jesus is acknowledged as a prophet (*Nabi*) many times in the Koran.[34] Of the twenty-five prophets mentioned in the Koran, none get the attention Jesus does in Islamic tradition. The Hadith adds accounts of His return on Judgment Day to the Koran's material on His virgin birth, life, and particular role. Not even Muhammad, who is considered the final and perfect prophet of Allah, is considered to have the unique qualities that Jesus has in the Koran.[35]

In line with His prophetic mission, Jesus is also known as a messenger (*Rasul*) of Allah.[36] There is no clear difference, according to Islamic theology, between being a messenger and being a prophet, although somehow not every messenger is a prophet but every prophet is a messenger. Still, every prophet is nothing more than a slave of Allah.

35. So despite giving Jesus such high regard, Muslims believe him to be a "slave of Allah?"

Yes, the Koran calls Jesus the servant or slave of Allah (*Abdullah: Abd* is slave, and *Allah,* of course, is God) in Suras 4:172, 19:30, and 43:59. This is one of the most frequently used titles accorded to Jesus by Muslims when they wish to proselytize Christians: by saying that Jesus was a "slave of Allah," they dismiss Christians' claims of Jesus' divinity. Calling Jesus a slave of Allah equates Him with all human beings because the master/slave relationship between Allah and Jesus also echoes the Islamic view of the relationship between Allah and mankind.

36. So Muslims would strongly disagree that Jesus and God are one and the same?

Absolutely. The Koran condemns those who consider Christ divine: "In blasphemy indeed are those that say that Allah is Christ the son of Mary" (Sura 5:17). Yet at the same time, Jesus is called the "Word of Allah" several times in the

Koran: "The angel said, 'Mary, Allah makes an announce-
ment to you of a word from himself whose name is the
Messiah, Jesus son of Mary, outstanding in this world and
the next, and one of those drawn near" (Sura 3:45). And
again in Sura 4:171: "The Messiah, Jesus son of Mary, is
only a messenger of Allah and a word which He projected
to Mary, and a spirit from Himself."

Related to this is a hint of the Christian doctrine that Jesus
is the New Adam: "The similitude of Jesus before Allah is
as that of Adam; He created him from dust, then said to
him: 'Be.' And he was" (Sura 3:59).

Islamic theologians throughout the history of Islam have
denied that the term "Word of Allah," as it is applied to
Jesus in the Koran, implies divinity. In line with Sura 3:59,
Muslims limit the meaning of a Divine "Word" to a command of Allah for something to come into existence. Yet in
so limiting the meaning, Muslims commit a basic linguistic
error. *Kelima* is the word used of Jesus as the Word of Allah,
but kelima does not mean "command" in Arabic. The word
for command is *amr;* kelima never has this meaning.

Muslim theologians, though, refuse to face the clear al-
ternative explanation: that the term is a fragment of Christian theology and can only be explained with reference to
Christ's divinity. Allah's "Word" is actually part of Him and
His divine nature, a manifestation of His divine essence. To
avoid this conclusion, Muslim scholars are forced to divide
Allah into many parts: His word, His spirit, His will, and
so forth. Yet this entangles Muslim theologians in a per-
ilous dalliance with notions that veer away from absolute
monotheism, and close to what Muslims themselves would
call blasphemy. Another hint of this comes in the Koran's
calling Jesus the "Spirit of God."

37. What does it mean that the Koran refers to Jesus as the "Spirit of God"?

In the Koran, Jesus is the Spirit of Allah: "O People of the Book! Commit no excesses in your religion: Nor say of Allah aught but the truth. Christ Jesus the son of Mary was (no more than) a messenger of Allah, and His Word, which He bestowed on Mary, and *a spirit proceeding from Him*: so believe in Allah and His messengers" (Sura 4:171, emphasis added).

Muslims have never faced the implications of this title. Why they have not is obvious: how can God's Spirit be anyone or anything other than God Himself? The spirit is the life of a being. What being exists without its life or separate from its life? Logically and philosophically, anything that emanates (that is, proceeds) from God must be God Himself — He cannot emanate anything that is less than Him. In its affirmation of Jesus as "a spirit proceeding from" Allah, the Koran contains another tantalizing hint of the divinity of Christ.

Many Koranic texts about Jesus can only be explained fully by Christian theology. This is why Jesus Himself is the key to communicating the truth of the Gospel to Muslims. However, this is a route full of hurdles. Chief among these obstacles, besides the Koran's explicit denial of Christ's divinity, is its denial of the crucifixion.

38. Why don't Muslims believe that Jesus died on the Cross?

Simply because the Koran says He did not. Muslims believe that He was taken alive up to Heaven, never having tasted death. It would be wrong for Allah to allow one of His prophets to die in shame and humiliation, so Allah placed someone who looked like Jesus on the Cross. The

Jews thought they were actually killing Jesus, but actually the imposter was crucified: "they slew Him not nor crucified, but it appeared so unto them" (Sura 4:157). The denial of the crucifixion and death of Jesus is, of course, a complete innovation. This denial is in direct contradiction to the Gospel texts. In all four Gospels, Jesus' passion, death, and resurrection are clearly enunciated. These events are, moreover, attested to in the writings of various non-Christian and secular sources including the writings of the Jewish historian Josephus, the *Annals* of Tacitus, and others (see question 39). Jesus' death and resurrection are acts essential to His person, life, and mission — to deny them (or any one of them) is to alter our understanding of the reality of Jesus and render Him less than who He truly is.

39. How then do Muslims explain the biblical accounts of Jesus' passion and death?

Because the Koran says that "it appeared" to those present that Jesus was crucified (see Sura 4:157), some Muslims accept the Bible's accounts at face value, but they insist that the Gospel writers and their sources were in error about the identity of the man on the Cross. Some say that it was actually Judas, made to look like Jesus by Allah.

Others repeat the traditional Muslim assertion that the biblical accounts have been corrupted, a charge we will soon examine in detail. Suffice it to say at this point that this charge flies in the face of a great deal of evidence. There are no non-Islamic sources to support the idea that Jesus was not crucified. On the Christian side, the historical evidence for the crucifixion is overwhelming. Christians do not even need to cite biblical sources to prove the crucifixion of Jesus occurred. Secular sources include Tacitus, in Book XV of his chronicle *The Annals of Imperial Rome*; Suetonius' *Life*

of the Emperor Claudius; Pliny, the governor of the Province
of Bithynia-Pontus, in book ten of his *epistles*; and Josephus,
the great Jewish historian, in his *Jewish Antiquities*.

The Koran does contain some hints that Jesus died at
some point. Sura 19:23 quotes the infant Jesus: "Peace be on
me the day I was born, the day I will die, and the day I am
risen back alive." The sequence here logically requires that
Jesus' death will follow His life on earth, then will come
His resurrection on Judgment Day.

The Koran also depicts Allah addressing Jesus about His
future death: "Jesus, I will cause you to die [*Mutawaffeka*]
and exalt you to My presence, and clear you of those who
disbelieve and make those who follow you above those who
disbelieve till the Day of Judgment" (Sura 3:55).

Some Muslim theologians, both past and present, take this
verse to mean that He was taken up to Heaven after Allah
caused Him to die. "Cause you to die" is the correct meaning
of *Mutawaffeka;* however, some Muslim translators render
this phrase as "take you to Myself."

This is because the linguistically correct understanding
creates problems in Islamic theology: it would mean Jesus
would die *two* deaths. For according to the Hadith, Jesus
will return to earth at the end of the age: "He will fight
the people for the cause of Islam. He will break the cross,
kill swine, and abolish jizyah. Allah will perish all religions
except Islam. He will destroy the Antichrist and will live on
the earth for forty years and *then he will die*. The Muslims
will pray over him [emphasis added]."[37] The idea that Jesus,
not Muhammad, will return is, of course, another hint of
the Christian theology that underlies so much of what Islam
teaches about Christ.

But if He dies at the end of the age, how could He have
died long before, at the end of His earthly life? To avoid this
difficulty, some Muslim commentators suggest that He has

not yet actually died, but has been taken up to Heaven alive. As we have seen, however, this is hard to defend in light of the words of the Koran: *Mutawaffeka* (literally, "cause to die") cannot mean "assumed to Heaven alive." It always refers to actual physical death. Elsewhere the Koran quotes Allah saying to Jesus, "Therein [that is, on earth] shall you live, and therein shall you die, and there from shall you be raised" (Sura 7:25).

Muslims say that Jesus was assumed into Heaven because Allah did not want Him to go through the pain and suffering that the Jews prepared for Him. Allah's Prophet could not suffer defeat. However, even according to the Koran, Allah allowed previous prophets to endure persecutions and suffering, all of them dying at the hands of the Jews (see Sura 2:61). Why should Jesus be spared such sufferings if he too was a prophet?

40. I have heard that Muslims have a high regard for Mary. Why is this?

Islam's high regard for Mary is rooted in various texts of the Koran, including the following: "Behold! the angels said: 'O Mary! Allah has chosen you and purified you — chosen you above the women of all nations'" (Sura 3:42).[38] The purity of Mary in Islamic thought is equated with sinlessness. This is echoed in the Hadith, where Muhammad says, "Every person to whom his mother gives birth [has two aspects of his life]; when his mother gives birth Satan strikes him but it was not the case with Mary and her son [Jesus Christ]."[39] The Koran even affirms the Virgin Birth of Jesus, echoing Mary's response to the angel Gabriel from St. Luke's Gospel: "She said: 'O my Lord! How shall I have a son when no man hath touched me?'" (Sura 3:47).

Muslim theologians, however, do not explore the implications of Mary's sinlessness or the Virgin Birth. They do not want to pursue a line of thought that might lead to the affirmation that Jesus was divine, a very disturbing conclusion for the Muslim. If Jesus could be shown to be divine, then the entire foundation of Islam (that is, Allah's revelations to Muhammad in the Koran) crumbles under the weight of such a truth. Why should God need to reveal Himself and His truth to Muhammad when he had already come in the person of the God-Man, Jesus?

The Koran's narratives about Mary and Jesus Christ are mixtures of legends, apocrypha, and certain canonical books. There is even confusion between Miriam, the sister of Moses and daughter of Amram (see Num 26:59), and Mary, the Mother of Jesus. Both names are *Maryam* in Arabic, and Muhammad seems to have thought that Jesus was Moses' nephew, the son of his sister. Jesus' Mother is addressed as "Sister of Aaron," the brother of Moses (Sura 19:28). St. Ann, Mary's mother, is even called the wife of Amram (see Sura 3:35). In fact, there were 1,500 years between these two Maryams. This obvious historical blunder should be a source of great consternation and difficulty for the Muslim apologist. If the Koran is so obviously mistaken on this point, why should it be considered reliable on other points of history?

41. Does Islam have a teaching authority similar to the Pope and Bishops?

No, but there are several notable sources that are considered authoritative in Islam. None of these sources, though, has a definitive authority similar to the Magisterium — that is, the Pope and the Bishops — of the Catholic Church. It is important for Christians to be aware of these sources of authority in Islam because occasionally they will affect how an individual Muslim understands a particular passage of the Koran or the Hadith. These authoritative sources include:

a. A *consensus* (Ijma') *of Islamic scholars*: if scholars agree on a disputed matter, their opinion carries much greater weight in an Islamic community than does the word of just one scholar.

b. The method of *reasoning by analogy (Qiyas).*

c. The *Sharia*, the classic Islamic legal system (which is the law of the land today in fundamentalist Muslim states) that emphasizes recourse to sources *(usul)* in dealing with matters of faith. *Usul al-fiqh*, or the methodology of sources in Islamic jurisprudence, is a highly developed study of proof texts from the Koran and the Hadith that are at the foundations of Islamic particular law.

All of these sources of authority are based firmly on the Koran, but the individual Muslim is still faced with the problem of the lack of a final, authoritative human interpreter of the Koran's teachings.

42. Is the Koran the sole rule of faith for the Muslim?

Not precisely. Muhammad's Tradition, the Hadith, is the second source of the Islamic faith. In Muslim theory and practice, the Hadith is virtually equal in importance to the Koran. Indeed, since Allah refers to many matters with which Muhammad is familiar but we are not, the Koran is often unintelligible. Muslims, however, are not free to interpret their sacred book in any way they please, for "whenever Allah and His apostles have decided a matter, it is not for the faithful man or woman to follow a course of their own choice" (Sura 33:36).

Muslims can find Muhammad's own authoritative explanations of passages of the Koran in a number of voluminous collections of *Ahadith* (Ahadith is the Arabic plural of Hadith). The Koran also commands every Muslim to follow Muhammad's example, obeying all that he did, said, commanded, or prohibited (see Sura 33:21).[40]

43. Is this "Islamic tradition" similar to Sacred Tradition as taught by the Catholic Church? If not, how do they differ?

The casual observer might see in the Islamic Hadith a curious similarity to the Catholic concept of Sacred Tradition, yet upon further investigation, this similarity proves to be superficial at best. While the Muslim has authoritative written traditions to aid him in interpreting the Koran, the Catholic has a teaching Church as the final authority in understanding God's revelation to man (see 1 Tm 3:15). Also, in Catholic understanding, Sacred Scripture and Sacred Tradition form one revelation, one "deposit of faith" (see CCC 84, 97). "Sacred Tradition" for Catholics refers to elements of the revealed Word of God that were not written down (see 1 Cor 11:2; 2 Thess 2:15; CCC 81, 83). As such, its elements are just as important as the teachings of the Bible, the written Word of God, because both the Bible and Tradition come from the same source — God Himself (see CCC 80). In Islam, this is generally not the case: the Hadith record the words and deeds of Muhammad, which are exemplary for Muslims but do not have the status of divine revelation, although some Muslims believe the Hadith was inspired by Allah.

There are, however, a small number of Traditions known as *Hadith Qudsi* (Sacred Hadith). These are Ahadith of divine origin that are not included in the Koran. They consist of Muhammad reporting words of Allah, and so are more analogous to Catholic Sacred Tradition since they have virtually the same standing for Muslims as the Koran itself. The Hadith Qudsi are so named because, unlike most of the Hadith, their authority is traced back not to Muhammad, but to Allah Himself.

As we have said, the Hadith collections contain the words and deeds of Muhammad, as well as his explanations of the Koranic revelations and his thoughts on a wide variety of doctrinal, ethical, legal, and historical matters. Many of these traditions are tales and stories from Muhammad's life, from which Muslims extract guidance on what to believe or how to behave in particular situations. Because of the Koran's command to imitate Muhammad, the overwhelming majority of Muslims consider the Hadith definitive and binding for all Muslims.

However, even though the Hadith is so highly regarded, the historical veracity of much of it is in dispute. There are many reasons for this. Although Muhammad lived in the early part of the seventh century, the collection of his words and deeds was not completed until the ninth and tenth centuries. This is evident from certain Hadith that attribute statements to Muhammad that actually reflect social and economic conditions (as well as doctrinal disputes) of a much later period.[41]

44. **I have heard that some of the Muslim traditions are very strange, such as the idea that yawning is evil. Is this true?**

Yes. Many traditions of Muhammad are downright bizarre and reveal a strange mixture of superstition and folk religion, including the idea that yawning is evil. "The Prophet said, 'Yawning is from Satan and if anyone of you yawns, he should check his yawning as much as possible, for if anyone of you (during the act of yawning) should say: *"Ha"*, Satan will laugh at him.' "[42]

This is not the only odd belief contained in Islamic tradition. Consider these examples as well:

"The Prophet said, 'If anyone of you rouses from sleep and performs the ablution, he should wash his nose by putting water in it and then blowing it out thrice, because Satan has stayed in the upper part of his nose all the night.' "[43]

"The Prophet said, 'Do not kill snakes except the short-tailed or mutilated-tailed snake with two white lines on its back, for it causes abortion and makes one blind. So kill it.' "[44]

"The Prophet said, 'Angels do not enter a house which has either a dog or a picture in it.' "[45]

45. Doesn't Islam also teach that dark skin is some sort of curse or penalty?

Unfortunately yes. The tradition you refer to is particularly ironic in light of Islam's rapid growth among African Americans: "Muhammad said, 'When Allah created Adam, He hit Adam on the right shoulder and the white race sprang out, while the black race came from the left shoulder. Allah said to those of the right hand to Paradise you are and to the left to hell you go.' "[46] This may be based on Sura 3:106: "On the Day when some faces will be [lit up with] white, and some faces will be [in the gloom of] black: To those whose faces will be black, [will be said]: 'Did ye reject Faith after accepting it? Taste then the penalty for rejecting Faith.' "

Muslim apologists have attempted to soften these harsh words by pointing to other Koranic teachings that all humans come from Adam and Eve (Sura 49:13) and that skin colors and races are seen by Allah as good (see Sura 30:22). In addition, Muhammad proclaimed racial equality in his

Last Sermon. Nevertheless, the offending traditions mentioned above remain problematic.

46. How do Muslims know that the traditions about Muhammad are true?

In the first two centuries after Muhammad's death, false traditions about him proliferated. Many early Muslims seem to have invented Ahadith to justify their positions on Islamic doctrine, law, or practice. Ultimately the situation became so confusing that Muslim scholars began to take pains to determine which stories were authentic and which were not. The result was the general acceptance of six collections of Hadith that are called *Sahih Sittah*, or Authentic Compilations. The most important of these is the *Sahih Bukhari* — Sahih means "authentic," and Bukhari is the name of the man who compiled this collection. Though he lived in the ninth century, nearly two hundred years after Muhammad, Bukhari was the most eminent pioneer in collecting and classifying the Hadith. (Bukhari is referenced throughout this book.)

One of the chief functions of the Hadith and the schools of jurisprudence is to make sense of the Koran's contradictory teachings on various matters.

47. Are there contradictions in the Koran? If so, then how can Muslims believe that it is inspired?

In fact, there are so many contradictions that it became necessary over the centuries for Muslim scholars to develop a system for their adherents to maintain their faith in the face of logical and compelling apologetics by non-Muslims. Some of the difficulties in the Koran are dealt with by the "nullification theory," a convenient method of altering teachings that appear illogical or confusing. Muslim theologians have devoted years to sorting out which parts of the Koran are actually the Word of Allah to be recited and followed, and which verses have been abrogated (that is, denied at a later date) by Allah Himself.

The Muslim circumvents the potential negative impact of self-contradictory verses in the Koran by insisting that Allah simply does not have to be consistent. In fact, consistency would be a limitation of His absolute freedom and power. A Muslim will say, "Allah is Divine, and can say and do whatever He likes. It does not matter that what He says seems not to make sense to us: we are only human and He is God. If Allah wishes to nullify what He said at an earlier time, He has every right to do so. He can deny His previous word in order to improve or change whatever He pleases. Even on a whim, Allah can change His mind, and say something completely opposite to His earlier word!"

The Koran even declares that the author of some of the abrogated verses is none other than the Prince of Darkness: "Never have We sent a single prophet or apostle before you with whose wishes Satan did not tamper. But Allah abrogates the interjections of Satan and confirms His own revelations. Allah is all-knowing and wise" (Sura 22:52).

Some of these interjections of Satan seem to appear in the Koran itself. Take, for example, the Koran's varying injunctions about alcohol. In Sura 2:219, Allah says to Muhammad, "They ask you about drinking and gambling. Say: 'There is great harm in both, although they have some benefit for men; but their harm is greater than their benefit.'"

Yet another verse makes it questionable in the extreme that there could be "some benefit for men" in alcohol, for it is one of Satan's tricks: "Believers, wine and games of chance . . . are abominations devised by Satan" (Sura 5:90). Why would the Evil One devise something that was of any benefit at all to mankind? Because of this anomaly, Sura 2:219 is generally considered to have been abrogated.

But even that is not all that is curious about the Koran's teachings on alcohol. What is beyond amazing is that believers will enjoy this "abomination devised by Satan" in Heaven: "This is the Paradise which the righteous have been promised. Therein shall flow . . . rivers of wine delectable to those that drink it" (Sura 47:15; see also 83:25–26).

A very serious example of verses being "nullified by Allah" is the instance when Muhammad apparently made an exception to his radical monotheism. During the early stages of Islam, Muhammad was frustrated in his attempts to win over Mecca's merchants and other powerful people, who were all polytheists. Finally he relented on his hitherto uncompromising monotheism and stated that it was permitted for the pagan gods of Mecca — specifically, three female deities named al-Lat, al-Uzza, and Manat — to intercede before Allah for the people. According to Islamic tradition, Satan took advantage of Muhammad's desire for reconciliation and "put upon his tongue" as a revelation from Allah this rhetorical question and answer: "Uzza and Manat, the third, the other? These are the exalted Gharaniq [cranes] whose intercession is approved." The pagan members of Muhammad's tribe, the Quraysh, were pleased; they prostrated themselves before their gods as the Muslims were prostrating themselves before Allah, and went out saying, "Muhammad has spoken of our god in splendid fashion."

Soon though, Gabriel came to Muhammad and scolded him, stating that Muhammad had taught something false. Allah then revealed that Satan routinely tampers with the messages of the prophets (see Sura 22:51), and that He later annuls these demonic interpolations.[47] This is the notorious Satanic Verses incident. These verses became familiar to

Western non-Muslims when novelist Salman Rushdie used this incident as a springboard for his novel *The Satanic Verses* — earning himself a death sentence for blasphemy from Iran's Ayatollah Khomeini.

In considering all these Koranic contradictions, a Catholic would contend that an all-knowing, all-powerful God cannot contradict Himself (see Heb 6:17–18). Such a concept is logically absurd. Since God exists outside of space and time, all reality is eternally present to Him — so, strictly speaking, God cannot "change His mind" because change implies time, something that God does not "have." God's will and decrees should therefore be seen as eternal and unchanging law because they are rooted in His very nature.

48. How then can Muslims claim that the Koran is the word of Allah, sent down from Heaven and preserved by the divine hand from corruption?

Because Allah says so. The nullification theory was not devised by Muslim theologians; it comes from the Koran. In Sura 2:106, Allah acknowledges that He cancels verses and substitutes new revelations for old ones: "If We [Allah] abrogate a verse or cause it to be forgotten, We will replace it by a better one or one similar." Elsewhere He takes note of Muhammad's critics: "When We change one verse for another (Allah knows best what He reveals), they say, "You [Muhammad] are an imposter. Indeed most of them have no knowledge" (Sura 16:101). Ultimately, it is a matter of the inscrutable divine will: "Allah abrogates and confirms what He pleases" (Sura 13:39).

Clearly the nullification theory was developed because of contradictions in Muhammad's message. Whatever its original intention, however, this technique has today become a convenient instrument that Muslims often use to sidestep Christian apologetic efforts. Nullification makes it virtually useless for Christians to point out contradictions in the Koran, and effectively blunts the impact of an appeal to Deuteronomy 18:22, which directs the Israelites "not to be afraid" of a prophet whose words are proven false.

A table of some of the Koran's doctrinal self-contradictions, large and small, appears at the end of this book. These self-contradictions do not carry the weight in Islam that a Christian might expect, however. A logical understanding of Allah and His word are not of much importance to a Muslim. Odd as it may seem, a Muslim is not nearly as concerned as is a committed Christian with whether or not his faith makes sense; his primary concern is with whether or not he (and all mankind) submits to Allah's will.

If we work out the logical consequences of the idea of nullification, we arrive at numerous conclusions that make Muslims uncomfortable. Even heretical Muslim sects have defended themselves using the nullification theory, maintaining that it proves that despite the claims of orthodox Muslim, the Koran is not necessarily the final revelation of Allah. After all, can He not do whatever He likes and change anything He has said in the past? He could even require Muslims tomorrow to become believers in the Trinity and join the Catholic Church! If Allah Himself is not immutable and unchangeable, or even loyal to the truth, then we must acknowledge that when He revealed the Koran, He meant little or nothing of what He says about Himself, or His prophets and Books, for this information is subject to revision or outright nullification.

Indeed, some say that the nullification theory proves that Allah had no obvious purpose in mind when He recited certain verses in the Koran to Muhammad. Before He was finished revealing His words to the prophet, He said other, contradictory things — serving only to confuse man's attempts to understand Him.

To allege that God has no need to adhere to the truth is to say that God can be a liar. For Christians this is not only blasphemy, it is an impossibility. God cannot deny Himself. He *is* Truth (see Jn 14:6). He does not speak something false to mankind and ask us to obey it. He could not rightly ask us to obey Him if He were untrustworthy. The Catholic faith, therefore, can point to the unchanging nature of its own doctrine as proof of its definitive, divinely-revealed character.

Not only does the nullification theory oppose logic and sound theology; it also contradicts the Koran itself. For in it, we read: "Such was the way of Allah in days gone by: and you shall find no change in the ways of Allah" (Sura 48:23). A similar proclamation is made in Sura 6:115: "Perfected are the words of your Lord in truth and justice. None can change His words." It is also in Sura 17:77: "Such were our ways with the apostles whom we sent before you [Muhammad]. You shall find no change in our way." A Hadith echoes this: "My Word does not change," Allah says flatly.[48] But the nullification theory holds that Allah's word does change.

Mutability is a manifestation of imperfection. Can the Koran then be giving a true picture of the Almighty God who is perfect in all things? Abrogation and nullification are not the same as a progressive understanding of divine revelation: it is one thing to gradually understand more and more of God's revelation to humanity (as in the Catholic faith), but it is entirely another to change the substance of the revelation to its opposite.

The plain fact of the case is that whole idea of abrogation demonstrates that the Koran is merely a human book.

49. Are there historical mistakes in the Koran?

For a Muslim, such an idea is inconceivable. If Allah changes His mind and abrogates a verse, or if He cancels a verse inspired by Satan, that is one thing. But an error about a matter of fact is another. In the Koran itself, Allah proclaims this is impossible: "This is a mighty scripture. Falsehood cannot reach it from before or from behind" (Sura 41:41–2). It is "free from any flaw" (Sura 39:28). In short, "it is the indubitable truth" (Sura 69:51).

Yet, in fact, the Koran contains many historical errors. For example, it claims that Alexander the Great was a Muslim in the story of *Zul-qarnain* (Sura 18:89–98), whom Muslim exegetes both ancient and modern identify as Alexander. Such appropriation of historical figures might be understandable in the case of a figure like Abraham, but Alexander was not even a monotheist.

In its retelling of the adventures of Moses and Aaron in Pharaoh's court, the Koran has Pharaoh threatening his magicians with crucifixion, a punishment that was not devised until centuries later — and then by the Romans, not the Egyptians.[49] Elsewhere, a Samaritan is said to have helped the Israelites to build the Golden Calf (Sura 20:90). It is an established historical fact that Samaria did not exist prior to the existence of Israel. The Golden Calf episode, of course, took place in the wilderness at Mount Sinai *before* the Israelites entry into the Promised Land (see Ex 32).

The Koran also claims that John the Baptist was the first person named John (see Sura 19:7), an assertion that is refuted in the Old Testament (see 1 Kgs 25:23, 1 Chron 3:15, and elsewhere) and many other ancient documents. Muslim apologists defend the Koran by claiming that the Arabic name *Yahya* does not correspond to the Hebrew and Greek words for John, but this is specious: Zechariah's son is universally known only as *John* the Baptist.

Two of the Koran's most egregious historical errors, as we have seen, involve Christianity: it confuses the family of Mary and Jesus with the family of Moses and Aaron, and it denies the crucifixion of Jesus Christ — an event which, as we have discussed earlier (see question 39), is well-documented in ancient non-Christian historical sources.

50. Aren't there similar contradictions or historical errors in the Bible?

Many Muslims (and non-Muslims as well) purport to find such contradictions in the Bible. Some of these "contradictions" are simple misunderstandings of the genres and writing styles of the Scriptures; others are more substantive and draw the attention of serious scholars. If understood correctly, however, the Bible can be shown to be without error in all those matters God wished to reveal for our salvation (see CCC 107). Thus, strictly speaking, no true contradictions (only *apparent* contradictions) exist in the Sacred Scriptures.

In dialogue with Muslims, though, it is never profitable to get into a "Scripture-error match." Many of these perceived errors are based on assumptions and presuppositions. In any case, Catholics should guard against the temptation to equate the Bible and the Koran, however favorable the comparison may be to the Bible.

As many Christians have remarked, the closest analogy to the Koran, as understood by Muslims, is not the Bible but the Person of Jesus Christ, the Word of God. No list of Bible contradictions, however superficially compelling, should damage the faith of a Catholic. Our faith is not in a book, but in a Person and in the Church He founded. The Bible did not make the Church; the Church compiled the Bible, and a Catholic should draw not just upon the Bible but upon the entire Tradition of the Church in explaining and defending his faith.

51. Has Islamic belief or doctrine changed over the centuries?

Not in any significant way. The simplicity of Islamic theology makes large-scale doctrinal upheavals (on the scale of the early Church's Christological controversies, for example) unusual in Islam. But this is not to say that there have been no doctrinal disagreements in the Islamic world.

One of the first and greatest of these was not originally a disagreement over doctrine but, in many ways, has evolved into one. After Muhammad died, the Muslim community chose his companion Abu Bakr to succeed him as Caliph, or leader of the Muslims. But one party of Muslims thought that the leadership belonged by right to Ali, Muhammad's son-in-law. This is the origin of the great split in Islam between the Sunnis and the Shi'ites. The Shi'ites believe that only a descendent of Muhammad could succeed him. Over the centuries Shi'ites, the dominant Muslim sect in Iran and parts of Iraq, elaborated doctrines and practices that differ in many ways from the Sunni Islam that is dominant in the rest of the Islamic world.

Still, for the most part there has been unity on the chief points of Islamic doctrine. Muslims point proudly to this unity, which they say contrasts with the way in which Jews and Christians have changed the Bible.

52. Why do Muslims believe that Jews and Christians have changed the Bible?

The Koran declares that the Gospel contains "guidance and light" and that the Torah is "a guide and an admonition to the righteous" (Sura 5:46). But because the Old and New Testaments do not agree with the Koran, most Muslims do not identify the Torah and the Gospel referred to in the Koran with today's Old and New Testaments. For Muslims, the "Torah" and the "Gospel" were books that were virtually identical to the Koran; Allah gave the former to Jews through the prophet Moses, and the latter to Christians through the prophet Jesus. Of course, this idea of the Gospel as a book given to Jesus is fundamentally different from the Christian idea of the Gospel as a message, not as a single book — a message *about* Jesus Christ, not delivered *to* Him.

Muslims believe that what Christians and Jews call their Sacred Scriptures are not the originals. When Muslims assert that they believe in the Torah and the Gospel, they are actually declaring their belief in books that they consider to have been eradicated from the earth. (It is important to remember, though, as a matter of historical fact, that neither the Torah nor the Gospel existed as single "books" in the first place. In fact, the New Testament as we know it was not definitively collected and established by the Church until the fourth century.) According to Islamic belief, the "original" and "uncorrupted" Torah and Gospel foretold the coming of Muhammad as the final prophet. Muslims do not believe that any copies of this "true Bible" exist today.

Muslims believe that ancient Jewish and Christian scholars long ago conspired to collect every copy of their Sacred Scriptures. They believe that the scholars then altered the ancient Scriptures, deleting the name of Muhammad and the prophecies indicating that Allah would send the final prophet. Muslims also believe that doctrines like the Trinity and the death of Jesus on the cross are blasphemous fabrications that were added to the Bible by devious men. This adulteration of Holy Scripture, Muslims claim, served the purposes of the Jews and Christians who wanted to reject Muhammad and keep their own positions secure. They believe that Jews and Christians cared so little for God that they changed the Word of Allah and lost the covenant Allah had made with them, thus passing this covenant to the Arab nation. The Koran and Hadith state that the tampering with the Bible was accomplished by changing the *meaning* of the Scriptures and changing the *text* of the Scriptures. All this keeps most Muslims from ever reading the Bible. Why read a book that is merely a Jewish-Christian fiction?

This is also one reason why many fanatical Muslims hate Jews and Christians — and why we are called infidels. The average Muslim believes that Jews and Christians are under a curse for changing their Scriptures: "Because of their breaking the Covenant, We [Allah] have cursed them and made hard their hearts. They changed words from their places and have abandoned a good part of the Message that was sent to them. And you will not cease to discover deceit in them, except a few of them. But forgive them and overlook. Verily! Allah loves the kindly" (Sura 5:13).

Muslims throughout history have demanded that Jews and Christians accept the Koran's assertions that both Christians and Jews lost favor with Allah because they tampered with the revelations that Allah gave to them.

Of course, this did not happen and could not have happened. In the first place, we have copies of large portions of the Old Testament and the entire New Testament that date from long before the time of Muhammad. With some minor textual variations that do not affect essential doctrines, these ancient manuscripts are the same as the versions we have today. This in itself gives lie to the assertion they were corrupted.

The corruption charge also defies common sense. No "original" (that is, "uncorrupted") fragments of Old or New Testament texts exist that corroborate this charge. In addition, it would have been geographically impossible for such a conspiracy to succeed, since there were innumerable copies of the Old and New Testaments all over the world, and no one would possibly have been able to find and gain possession of all of them. Many of them were in the hands of desert monks who had little or no communication with the outside world. How such an organized "corruption campaign" could take place in a world without mass communication, separated by mountains and oceans, among men of different races, languages, and religions, is never adequately explained by Muslims.

The care with which Jews and Christians treated the Scriptures also testifies against the idea of corruption. Catholic (and later Orthodox) religious orders designated scribes whose sole task in life was to transcribe the entire Bible by hand. These holy monks were scrupulously careful not to alter one line of Scripture. The manual copying of the Old Testament went on for much a longer period than did that of the New Testament, but here again there are numerous indications that it was done with tremendous care. The discoveries of the Dead Sea Scrolls confirm that the Old Testament we have today is identical with that of two thousand years ago and more, and that in centuries of manual transmission no significant alterations occurred, even of a single line.[50]

Indeed, the reverential attitude of Jewish priests and scribes toward the Name of God (*Yahweh*, a word related to the designation "I Am who Am" in Ex 3:14) indicates the respect in which they held Scripture. They were in such awe of God that they would not pronounce His Name, so that ultimately the vowels were lost: the Hebrew alphabet contained only consonants. Even today pious English-speaking Jews write "G-d" rather than "God." This reverence makes it outlandish to think that they would have dared to corrupt the Scriptures on such a grand scale as Muslims envision.

Yet despite the absence of proof and the logical difficulties involved with the idea that the Jewish and Christian Scriptures were corrupted, Muslims continue to insist that they were. The chief reason given in the Koran for why Jews and Christians changed the Scriptures is a desire for material gain: "Woe to them that write the Scriptures with their own hands and then declare, 'This is from Allah' in order to gain some paltry end" (Sura 2:79). This text suggests that Jews and Christians would invent "Scripture" in order to sell it for a profit.

53. Does Islam believe in the intercession of saints or angels?

Some forms of saintly or angelic intercession are generally accepted, but others are not.

Regarding accepted intercession, the Koran notes: "No intercession is accepted by Allah except by His permission" (Sura 2:255). The Koran gives no clear indication of what kind of intercession Allah actually permits, although most Muslim sects acknowledge and permit the practice of calling upon Muhammad for intercession.

In terms of rejected forms of intercession, Muslims reject the invocation of angels, prophets, or saints on the basis of Koranic verses like this one: "Almighty Allah does not command you to take the angels and prophets as Lords" (Sura 3:80). The Koran rejects the distinction between worship and asking for prayer: "They serve beside Allah beings which can neither benefit nor harm, claiming, 'These are our intercessors with Allah'" (Sura 10:18).

As mentioned, some Muslims call upon Muhammad as an intercessor. Yet they leave unexplained why it is acceptable to ask for Muhammad's intercession but not that of any other prophet. According to the thinking of most Muslims, asking anyone other than Muhammad to pray for you is equivalent to an act of worship, and is therefore idolatry. Thus Muslims frown on the Christian practice of calling upon Jesus, as well as Mary and other saints. They point to the Koran's denial of Christ's divinity to justify this: "And Allah said to Jesus, son of Mary: 'Did you ask men to take you and your mother for objects of worship beside Almighty Allah?' He answered: 'Praise be to You, O Allah! How can I have asked that which is not mine to ask?'" (Sura 5:116).

54. How does the Muslim view of Allah differ from the Christian understanding of God?

The Koran's picture of Allah is radically different from the God of the Bible. In the Bible, God is at once both transcendent and, to a certain extent, knowable. Muslims, however, believe that Allah is so far above His creation (including mankind) that He can never be known. Muslims will never "see God as He is," as St. John promises Christians will (1 Jn 3:2).

Even in Paradise, the blessed will not be with Him: in all of the Koran's notorious talk of the joys of Heaven, the presence of Allah is never mentioned. Allah will remain radically transcendent, unapproachable, and unknowable. Paradise is envisioned as offering only physical, sensory pleasures.

Islam generally rejects *anthropomorphic language* (that is, the use of human terms and experience to describe God and

His interactions with man) as inconsistent with Allah's transcendence. Although there are anthropomorphisms in the Koran, these are unacceptable in Islamic theology: "Whatever of good ye give benefits your own souls, and ye shall only do so seeking the 'Face' of Allah" (Sura 2:272; the quotation marks around the word "Face" indicate the Muslim translator's discomfort with the anthropomorphism). Allah is utterly and totally transcendent and has nothing in common with mankind. He cannot be spoken of in human terms.[51]

For Muslims, Allah is not viewed as a Father, but as a Master who orders His slaves to obey strict rules. He has no relationship with them on earth or in Heaven. Muslims obey His commands in order to gain entry into Paradise. The concepts of service to others motivated by divine love, and love for one's enemies, are Christian ideas that are foreign to Islam.

The concept of Allah's love in the Koran is tied to obedience. Allah's love is only for Muslims, as Allah hates unbelievers: "Allah is an enemy to those who reject faith" (Sura 2:98). The idea of a God who sacrifices Himself for us while we were His enemies is unique to Christianity: "But God demonstrates his own love for us in this: While we were still sinners, Christ died for us" (Rom 5:8).

55. What are the "99 Names of Allah" that we hear about?

Muslims claim that there are 99 Holy Names (or titles) for Allah. These are listed in the Hadith collection *Sunan Ibn Majah*.[52] These Holy Names of Allah are considered majestic (see Sura 55:78), and reciting them is said to be a source of grace and blessings (see Suras 7:180; 17:110; 20:8; and 59:24). In the homes of many Muslims, these Holy Names in Arabic script decorate the walls. Among the most popular of these Names are The Compassionate, The Merciful, The King, The Holy, and The Giver of Faith. Others include the The Strong, the The Almighty, The Majestic, The Creator, and The All-Knowing. ("The Loving" is not among these Names, however.) It is interesting to note, however, that although Muslims claim that all of these Names are in the Koran, only 73 can actually be found there. Muslims duplicate fifteen Names that are found in the Koran by listing them both in verb and noun forms; the remaining eleven names do not exist in the Koran at all. Other traditions say that Allah has 100 names, but only a camel knows the hundredth.[53]

Allah's Names are not to be understood as articulating anything about His nature. Islamic theologians claim that in the Koran Allah did not reveal His attributes, but only His commands. Muslims are called to obedience, not to hopeless attempts to understand or know Allah. Muslims insist that Allah is basically unknowable. His nature cannot be comprehended. In fact, speculating on Allah's nature is considered blasphemy, since it assumes that Allah is knowable.

This unknowable God is completely different from the loving Father of the Bible, who reveals His nature in the Trinity and His love in the Incarnation of His Son. A Catholic would counter the Muslim view of Allah's radical transcendence with the firm conviction that God wills us to know Him so that we might love Him. It is impossible to love someone you do not know. Naturally, because God is infinite and we are finite, we can never know Him fully. Yet even a partial knowledge of God and His love for us is enough to inflame our desire to love Him in return.

56. It would seem that Islam's significantly different view of God would have a serious effect on faith and practice. Could you comment on this?

One could note many examples of how misguided belief leads to misguided morality. False teachings about God and His nature can be the root of all sorts of false religious and social practices. In Islam, a distorted view of God (Allah) has led to several problems.

For example, seeing Allah as Slave Master (and we as His slaves) leads to a legalistic morality. The individual Muslim can only strive to obey Allah's arbitrary laws to be saved, and he can never hope for a loving relationship with a forgiving Father. This is not to say that Allah has no love for the faithful Muslim believer (see Sura 2:195; 3:148; and others), only that the believer is incapable of having any true relationship with Him; Allah remains transcendent Master. With such a view of God, it is not difficult to see why the practice of slavery itself would be tolerated under such a religious system.

57. Do Muslims believe they worship the same God as Jews and Christians?

No, Muslims believe they worship a different God, or at least, that their understanding of God is different from that of Jews and Christians. This is despite certain Koranic texts which claim that the God of Judaism and Christianity is the same as Allah of the Muslims: "Say: It is only inspired in me that your Allah is One Allah. Will ye then surrender [unto Him]?" (Sura 21:108). That he is addressing Christians and Jews is made clear by another verse: "And do not dispute with the followers of the Book except by what is best, except those of them who act unjustly, and say: We believe in that which has been revealed to us and revealed to you, and our Allah and your Allah is One, and to Him do we submit" (Sura 29:46).

Even still, Muslims vehemently deny that the Allah of the Koran is the God of the Bible. Not only is the very notion of the Trinity blasphemous to Muslims, but referring to God as "Father" is for them blasphemous as well. Even to say such a thing would put a Muslim at risk of Hell. As we explained in some detail in question 54, Allah is not a Father who seeks our love but a Master who demands our obedience.

To an objective observer, then, it should be clear that the Allah of the Koran cannot be identified with the loving Father whom Christians worship.

58. Doesn't the *Catechism of the Catholic Church* teach that all religions (including Muslims) worship the one true God to a greater or lesser degree?

Not precisely. The *Catechism of the Catholic Church* says that "[t]he plan of salvation also includes those who acknowledge the Creator, in the first place amongst whom are the Muslims; these profess to hold the faith of Abraham, and together with us they adore the one, merciful God, mankind's judge on the last day" (CCC 841).

This is a carefully worded statement that warrants close examination.

"The first place amongst whom are the Muslims; these profess to hold the faith of Abraham." This statement is not saying that Muslims actually believe in Abraham's faith, but only that they *profess* to hold the faith of Abraham. Professing and possessing are two different things: for example, there are certainly many more Christians who profess Christ than there are people who actually live for Him.

"Together with us they adore the one, merciful God, mankind's judge on the last day." Again, this statement is very carefully worded: it does not say that Muslims adore the *same* merciful God, but only that, like us, "they adore the one merciful God." Strictly speaking, the *Catechism* simply does not address the question of whether Allah, as worshiped in Islam, is truly the same God revealed in the Old and New Testaments. It should be noted, however, that Pope John Paul II, commenting on this same *Catechism* citation, indicated in his May 5, 1999 general audience that Muslims and Christians believe in the same God (www.ewtn.com/library/papaldoc/jp2muslm.htm).

59. **As you have said in the previous answer, the Catechism teaches that God's plan of salvation includes Muslims. If this is true, then why should Catholics be concerned when people embrace Islam?**

As you note in your question, the *Catechism of the Catholic Church* and the Second Vatican Council do indeed teach that "the plan of salvation also includes those who acknowledge the Creator, in the first place amongst whom are the Muslims; these profess to hold the faith of Abraham, and together with us they adore the one, merciful God, mankind's judge on the last day."[54] But, of course, more should not be read into this statement than it intends.

Like Christianity, Islam is a missionary faith — it constantly seeks converts. Muslims today like to tell Christians that they revere Jesus and His Mother, and that Christians should likewise revere Muhammad. After the terrorist attacks of September 11, 2001, many Catholics spoke of our Christian duty to forge bonds of unity and charity with Muslims. Such bonds, they argue, rule out trying to gain converts from Islam. This view, however prevalent it may be among Catholics, is virtually nonexistent among Muslims.

The reverence Muslims profess to have for Jesus and Mary has never prevented Muslims from making converts of Catholics. Not to mention the fact that Christians face persecution today in many Muslim countries worldwide. In fact, it is likely that many more Catholics become Muslims each year than Muslims become Catholics. In light of the teaching of Vatican II and the *Catechism* (as well as of the whole of Catholic tradition), this is a profound loss for a human being: he is exchanging what is fully true for what could be understood as only partially true. Should Catholics not then preach the Gospel to Muslims — not in spite of the fact that they are somehow included in the "plan of salvation," but because of it?

To be unwilling to bring the Gospel of Christ to Muslims would be to fail to acknowledge its uniqueness and power. Those who invoke the *Catechism* must also reckon with the fact that in the *Catechism* itself the Church is "urged on by the love of Christ to proclaim the Good News everywhere in the world."[55] One of the stated aims of the Council, meanwhile, was to proclaim the Gospel "to every creature," so that "it may bring to all men that light of Christ which shines out visibly from the Church."[56]

If we really believe that we possess in Christ the fullness of the truth, and as St. Paul tells us, the Church is "the pillar and foundation of truth" (1 Tm 3:15), then it is an act of simple charity to proclaim the Gospel to all people, including Muslims. Furthermore, even if one never meets a Muslim, much less proclaims the Gospel to him, it is every Christian's duty to become informed about Islam since it (along with secularism) is the Church's chief and most energetic present-day rival for souls.

60. Why do Muslims think that Christians are polytheists (that is, they believe in more than one god)?

Christians confess Jesus Christ as the Son of the Eternal God. But the Koran strongly and repeatedly denies that Jesus is God's Son. "The Jews call Ezra the Son of God," claims the Koran, "and the Christians call Christ the Son of God. This is a saying from their mouth; they but imitate what the unbelievers of old used to say. Allah's curse be on them: how they are deluded away from the truth!" (Sura 9:30).

However, Muhammad did not really understand what the Christians of his day meant when they called Jesus "the Son of God." He thought that to claim God has a son would be tantamount to saying that God had a wife with whom He had sexual relations. Muhammad could conceive of the idea of divine sonship only in physical terms. In the Koran, the true believers insist that "we shall never join anything [in worship] with our Lord and exalted be the Majesty of our Lord, He has taken neither a wife, nor a Son" (Sura 72:2–3). The denial is elsewhere put in question form: "How can He have a Son, when He has no wife?" (Sura 6:101).

In line with this is Muhammad's misunderstanding of the Christian doctrine of the Trinity. In the Koran, the Trinity includes Allah, Mary, and Jesus: "And when Allah saith: O Jesus, son of Mary! Didst thou say unto mankind: Take me and my mother for two gods beside Allah? He saith: Be glorified! It was not mine to utter that to which I had no right. If I used to say it, then Thou knewest it. Thou knowest what is in my mind, and I know not what is in Thy Mind. Lo! Thou, only Thou, art the Knower of Things Hidden?" (Sura 5:116).

Muhammad thus presumably thought that Christians believed that Mary had become Allah's wife and had given

birth to their son, Jesus. Obviously, this crude physicality is
far from the actual Christian concepts of the Trinity and
the Incarnation. But the Koran rejects all this as polytheism
and denies the divinity of Christ: "O people of the Scripture!
Do not exceed the limits in your religion, nor say of Allah
aught but the truth. The Messiah [Jesus], son of Mary, was a
Messenger of Allah and His Word, which He bestowed on
Mary and a spirit created by Him; so believe in Allah and
His Messengers. Say not 'Three!' Cease! Better for you, for
Allah is One. Glory be to Him above having a Son" (Sura
4:171). And again: "They do blaspheme who say: 'Allah is
one of three in a Trinity,' for there is no god except One
God" (Sura 5:73).

Since these and other Koranic passages suggest that Christians worship three gods, most Muslims assume this to be
true, and dismiss Christian denials as stemming from dis-
honesty or ignorance.

The Muslim conception of monotheism is thus closer to
the Jewish concept of God than to that of Christianity. All
three religions acknowledge the unity and transcendence of
God; however, for Jews and Muslims, God is an absolute
unity. Because of the doctrines of the Trinity and the divinity
of Christ, many Muslims believe that they, along with the
Jews, are monotheists, while Christians are polytheists.

This idea is related to the Muslim belief that Islam was
the original religion of Abraham and the other patriarchs,
and that Jews and Christians later corrupted this pure religion.

61. Why do Muslims claim Abraham was the first Muslim?

Muslims consider Abraham to be the first and in many
ways the greatest example of faith, as do Christians and
Jews, but Muslims also use the figure of Abraham to posi-

tion themselves as the legitimate spiritual heirs of the Judeo-Christian tradition.

Their argument is based upon the assertion that at the time of Muhammad, Jews and Christians were in dispute as to which group Abraham belonged. This strange belief, which lacks any historical foundation, comes from the Koran:

> O People of the Book! why do you dispute about Abraham, when the Torah and the Gospel were not revealed till after him; do you not then understand? Behold! you are they who disputed about that of which you had knowledge; why then do you dispute about that of which you have no knowledge? And Allah knows while you do not know. Abraham was not a Jew nor a Christian but he was (an) upright (man), a Muslim, and he was not one of the polytheists. Most surely the nearest of people to Abraham are those who followed him and this Prophet [Muhammad] and those who believe and Allah is the guardian of the believers (Sura 3:65–68).

The renowned Islamic scholar and Koranic commentator Ibn Kathir (1302–1373) explains the occasion of this revelation:

> A group of Christians and a few Jewish rabbis were meeting with Muhammad when they disputed about Abraham. The Christian claimed Abraham was a Christian and the Jew said Abraham was a Jew . . . and because of that, the next day, Allah revealed to Muhammad that Abraham was neither, but instead a true believer, a Muslim. . . . The Torah came after Abraham and Christianity also came after Abraham, so how could he belong to either one. . . .[57]

Islamic tradition goes even farther in claiming Abraham as the father of Islam. In one Hadith, Muhammad explains that on the Day of Resurrection, "you will be gathered, barefooted, naked, and uncircumcised," but that "the first human being to be dressed on the Day of Resurrection will be [the Prophet] Abraham *Al-Khalil* [Beloved Friend of Allah]."[58] Presumably he has this honor because, despite Muslim claims of prophetic status for Adam and Noah as well, Abraham enjoys a status as the father of the faith in Islam that is similar to his position in Judaism and Christianity. Also, another Hadith has Muhammad speaking of his journey to Paradise. He meets the prophets and describes them to his companions, noting that "I saw Abraham whom I resembled more than any of his children did."[59]

On the basis of all this, it has become customary to call Judaism, Christianity, and Islam the "three great Abrahamic faiths." In reality, however, there is no genuine historical or theological connection between Abraham and Islam.

62. Don't Muslims trace their ancestry to Abraham's son Ishmael?

Yes. Muslims believe that after Sarah expelled Hagar and Ishmael from Abraham's house, Hagar and Ishmael settled in Mecca. Islam portrays Ishmael as adhering to the monotheism later preached by Muhammad.

Perhaps not surprisingly, Muslims believe that Ishmael, not Isaac, was Abraham's sacrificial son. They maintain that, in the course of their corruption of the Scriptures, the Jews changed the story of Abraham's sacrifice to suit their own purposes by claiming Isaac was the sacrificial son. Curiously, though the son to be sacrificed is not mentioned by name in the Koran, Isaac is mentioned right after the account of the sacrifice (see Sura 37:100–112).

63. What is Islam's view of the Jewish people?

Muslims consider the Jewish nation to have been chosen especially by Allah: "O Children of Israel! Call to mind the [special] favor which I bestowed upon you, and fulfill your covenant with Me as I fulfill My Covenant with you, and fear none but Me" (Sura 2:40).

However, the Jews lost this position to the Muslims, and as we have seen, were transformed into detested "apes and swine." In line with this, many Muslims today claim that Ishmael was the "righteous son" whom Abraham almost sacrificed. However, this idea makes nonsense of the divine promises (which appear in Islamic as well as in Christian sources) that the birth of this son would be miraculous. For most Muslim tradition holds that while Abraham was old when Ishmael was born, the boy's mother, Hagar, was a robust twenty-four years of age. But where is the miracle in a twenty-four-year-old woman conceiving a child, even if the father is old? Only if the sacrificial son were Isaac, the son of the aged Sarah, would these traditions of a miraculous birth (common to Muslims, Christians, and Jews) make sense.

In addition, the Islamic view creates historical problems: if the Jews lost their special position *before* Abraham's sacrifice, so that Ishmael was the chosen son instead of Isaac, what of Moses and the other Jewish prophets that Islam acknowledges? Clearly the Muslim idea that Ishmael supplanted Isaac is an anachronistic interpolation of a later situation into the biblical text. This is yet another attempt by Islam to position itself as the true modern-day version of both Judaism and Christianity.

64. Do Muslims, like Christians, believe that man is created in God's image?

No. Muslims tend to think of the word "image" solely in physical terms. They think that to assert this is to claim that God looks like a human being. Since Allah is not to be thought of as having any human qualities, this would be tantamount to blasphemy.

Christianity, in contrast, teaches that God's creation of man in His own image means that He imparted to mankind a dignity beyond that which He displayed elsewhere in creation. Humanity's created dignity is rooted in God's gifts of intelligence (reason) and free will, attributes of God Himself. To recognize that God created man in His own image is not to diminish His might, but to elevate it: it shows God's goodness toward man. Man's creation in God's image refers to the fact that God gave man a spirit so that he could commune with God, who is Spirit.

But Islamic theology wishes to elevate Allah by denigrating man. The Koran aims to show that humanity is immeasurably below divinity. Man's origin is in Allah, and all that he receives is from Allah, but he does not receive the dignity of Allah's image and likeness.

65. What does Islam teach about the fall of Adam and Eve?

This is a very important question because, just as with their teaching about Jesus Christ, the Koran's and Hadith's teachings about the sin of Adam and Eve raise many unresolved questions and bear unmistakable traces of Christian theology. Ultimately, the confusions and dead ends of Muslim teaching about Adam and Eve can only be explained by reference to Christian theology — a fact with enormous implications for any objective seeker of the truth who examines the Koran.

The story of the fall of Adam in the Koran is in many ways similar to the biblical account: "And We said, 'O Adam! Dwell you and your wife in Paradise and eat with pleasure from its fruits, whenever you want, but do not come near this Tree, lest you become of those who offend'" (Sura 2:35). Like the book of Genesis, the Koran states that Adam and Eve transgressed the decrees of Allah by eating the forbidden fruit: "But Satan misled them, expelled them from the place in which they were; and We said, 'Fall down each one of you a foe unto the other! There shall be for you on earth a habitation and provision for a time'" (Sura 2:36).

Except for the suggestion that Satan expelled Adam and Eve from the Garden, the Koran thus far is in line with biblical accounts of the Fall. But in other ways, Islam differs in doctrine substantially from both Judaism and Christianity on the fall of Adam and Eve. In Genesis, Adam blames Eve, and Eve blames the serpent: they do not take responsibility for their sin, nor do they repent. Through their action, sin came into the world, and death infected all the children of Adam and Eve.

According to the Koran, on the other hand, Adam does ask Allah for pardon, and Allah forgives him.[60] For Muslims, that is the end of the matter. There is no hint that Adam's sin affects the human race in general in any way. Muslims do not call Adam's sin "original sin," as do both Catholics and Protestants, but instead the "first" and the "forgiven" sin.

However, the Islamic denial of the consequences of Adam's sin raises questions about the Koranic account:

1. If Allah pardoned Adam and Eve, why did He expel them from the garden?

This expulsion in itself is unexplained if Allah accepted Adam's repentance. Even more pointedly, however, another version of the same story in the Hadith has Adam explicitly bearing responsibility for humanity's exile from Paradise: "Allah's Apostle said, 'Adam and Moses met, and Moses said to Adam "You are the one who made people miserable and turned them out of Paradise.'"[61] Clearly this assumes that the human race somehow shares in Adam's exile. So some idea of the fall of mankind exists in the Hadith, even though it is contradicted by some verses of the Koran.

2. Adam and Eve were naked after they sinned. They realized their nakedness and covered it. But if Allah had forgiven Adam, why did he still feel guilt?

Once Allah forgave Adam, he would again walk in the complete innocence he had before the Fall. But the Koran, like the Bible, shows the situation of mankind changing completely after Adam's sin: on the face of it, Adam and Eve were not restored to a state of grace.

3. Muhammad taught that "every human is a sinner by nature, and the best among sinners are those who repent." If every human being is a sinner by nature, did Allah create Adam's offspring as sinners or was there some kind of Fall?

Some verses of the Koran seem to denigrate Allah Himself by stating that man's imperfection comes from how he was created: "Indeed, man was created impatient" (Sura 70:19). Either Allah did hasty work in creating man, or He instilled a native defect.[62]

4. Why was Muhammad a sinner?

Abu Huraira said, "I heard Allah's Apostle [Muhammad] saying, 'There is none born among the offspring of Adam, but Satan touches it. A child therefore cries loudly at the time of birth because of the touch of Satan, except Mary and her child.'" Then Abu Huraira recited: "And I seek refuge with You for her and for her offspring from the outcast Satan ([Sura] 3.36)."[63]

This implies that Muhammad himself, the apex and seal of the prophets, was a sinner, for according to Islamic teaching only Mary and Jesus were exempt from the touch of Satan at birth. But why would Allah allow Satan to touch Muhammad and all other human beings? This notion only makes sense in light of the Christian understanding of the Fall. Muhammad also said, "Satan circulates in the body of Adam's offspring as his blood circulates in it."[64]

The fact that Muslims believe that Mary and Jesus were born sinless is the most telling indication of all that the Koran's teachings about Adam and Eve, and about sin in general, are garbled representations of Christian teaching.

66. Does Islam have a theology of salvation? If so, how does it differ from the Catholic view?

In Islam, only Muslims can be saved since the only religion accepted by Allah on Judgment Day will be Islam. "If anyone desires a religion other than Islam [submission to Allah], never will it be accepted of him; and in the Hereafter he will be in the ranks of those who have lost [all spiritual good]" (Sura 3:85).

In the Koran, judgment for Muslims proceeds according to the scales. If one's good deeds outweigh his bad deeds, he will enter Paradise; if they do not, he will enter Hell: "And as for those whose scale is light [with good deeds]: those are they who lose their souls because they used to wrong Our revelations" (Sura 7:9).

The Catholic faith has always rejected the notion that we can "earn" our salvation through good deeds. No finite, sinful creature can merit Heaven. It is only through faith in the saving life, death, and resurrection of the infinite God-Man, Jesus, can we have eternal life. Salvation is a gift that is merely accepted or rejected, but never earned. Of course, we must accept this gift of salvation by remaining in God's grace by avoiding serious sin. This grace impels us to good works. Accordingly, St. Paul's trenchant analysis of the impossibility of being saved through good works applies as much to Islam as it did to Pharisaic Judaism.

Many converts from Islam to Christianity have described the powerful impression it made upon them when they realized through reading St. Paul's epistles that Islam is just a system of laws; it offers no salvation.

67. Christians believe that God forgives all sins. Do Muslims share this belief, or are there any unforgivable sins in Islam?

There are three types of sin for which Allah will not forgive sinners:

a. *Attributing Partners to Allah.* "Allah will not forgive idolatry. He that serves other gods besides Allah has strayed far indeed" (Sura 4:116). Attributing partners to Allah is called *shirk.* This specifically includes praying to Jesus Christ, the Holy Spirit, the Virgin Mary, the saints, and the angels. All these forms of intercessory prayers are considered forms of blasphemy in Islamic theology. Islamic commentators, both classical and contemporary, state that such prayers are blasphemous and unforgivable.

b. *The Killing of a Believer.* Under no circumstances should a Muslim kill any other Muslim intentionally. "Whoever kills a believer purposefully, his reward is hell forever. Allah is wroth with him and hath cursed him and prepared for him an awful doom" (Sura 4:93). Numerous Muslim theologians agree that this sin cannot be forgiven. Non-Muslims may find this a curious belief given the numerous wars that have been fought between Muslim countries (for example, the seven-year-long Iran-Iraq War of the 1980s), and also given the terrorist attacks on the World Trade Center in which many Muslims were killed. The suicide terrorists of September 11, 2001 would certainly have known that fellow Muslims worked in those buildings.

c. *Apostasy.* "Lo! Those who disbelieve after their profession of belief, and afterward grow in infidelity, their repentance will never be accepted. And such are those who are astray" (Sura 3:90). The apostates include those who convert to another religion, as well as those who simply incline towards atheism. Islamic commentators indicate that the apostate multiplies his disbelief, and by persisting in it, adds further infidelity to disbelief.[65] Once he has become an apostate, he never actually regains the status of a believer even if he renounces his apostasy: an apostate is irrecoverably lost. One Hadith quotes Muhammad as listing three kinds of Muslims who may lawfully be killed by other Muslims: those who commit murder, those who commit adultery or other sexual crimes forbidden by Islamic law, and apostates.[66]

68. Does Allah call all people to embrace Islam?

No. This is a stunning departure from the God of the Bible who "wills all men to be saved and to come to the knowledge of the truth" (1 Tm 2:4).[67]

The Koran does not say why Allah chose not to guide all mankind to the truth, but about the fact that He did not is abundantly clear. There are over forty Koranic passages that deny free will. The conclusion is inescapable that Allah created a great many creatures defective and intended for Hell. Although some Islamic theologians state that man does nevertheless have free will, their claim is based on a limited selection of Koranic verses — especially those texts that mention disbelievers in Islam and stress their need to repent. The scholars use the notion of free will to avoid the unwelcome implications of the Koranic passages that depict Allah declining to guide people to the truth, and to argue that "infidels" are responsible for their choice to reject Allah and His prophet Muhammad. But free will is a relatively new idea in Islam, and lacks significant traditional support.

69. Is Allah, then, responsible for human sin?

In many verses, Allah is held responsible for the choices of individuals: in fact, some Ahadith suggest that Allah has actively devised sins for mankind. Says Muhammad: "Allah has written for the son of Adam his inevitable share of adultery whether he is aware of it or not. Another version of this Hadith puts it even more strongly: "Allah decreed that all humanity will have their share of adultery, whether they like it or not. . . ."[68]

Muslim apologists, in their attempts to win converts, ignore all this and try to convey the idea that there is free will and responsibility in Islam. One of the Koranic texts often used is Sura 36:67: "And if it had been Our Will, We could have transformed them [into animals or lifeless objects] in their places. Then they should have been unable to go forward, nor they could have turned back." The presumption is that men are now able to "go forward" or "turn back," that is, make choices for which they are responsible.

The bulk of the Koranic verses regarding a preordained human destiny, however, contradict such texts. Consider Sura 4:119: "And surely I will lead them astray, and surely I will arouse desires in them, and surely I will command them and they will cut the cattle's ears, and surely I will command them and they will change Allah's creation." The speaker here seems to be "those who call upon Satan," but the Koranic text is unclear: it could be Allah Himself. Does Allah arouse in the hearts of men vain desires and command them to tamper with His creation? It seems absurd that Allah could be saying and doing such things, but this seems precisely to be the case.

As the Koran states: "Those whom Allah [in His plan] wills to guide, He opens their breast to Islam; those whom He wills to leave straying, He makes their breast close and constricted, as if they had to climb up to the skies: thus does Allah [heap] the penalty on those who refuse to believe" (Sura 6:125). Allah even leaves sinners alone so that He can punish them all the more: "Let not the Unbelievers think that our respite to them is good for themselves: We grant them respite that they may grow in their iniquity: But they will have a shameful punishment" (Sura 3:178; see also Sura 11:34).

Sura 4:119 says, "He who chooses Satan rather than Allah for his protector ruins himself beyond redemption." How can this be true in light of the Koran's entire portrayal of Allah? Is this a picture of a "most merciful" and "most compassionate" God? Why would someone choose Allah as his protector if He arouses in him vain desires, leaves him with no guidance, and destines him for Hell? Why should one submit to a god who acts, in the words of the Koran, as "the best of plotters" (Sura 8:30)?

The God worshiped by Christians, however, never leads people to sin; His grace always impels us towards virtue and holiness. And, should we be tempted by the world, the flesh, or the Devil, God offers us sufficient grace to avoid sin (1 Cor 10:13).

70. What is the Islamic teaching on Paradise (Heaven)?

The Muslim concept of the afterlife in Paradise differs dramatically from the Christian view of Heaven as a blissful union with God Himself, a veritable partaking of the divine nature (see 2 Pt 1:4). In Islam, Allah remains unknowable even in Paradise. Humans will never be able to approach Him, know Him, or see Him.

For the "single-minded slaves of Allah" there is "a known provision, fruits. And they will be honored in the Gardens of delight, on couches facing one another; a cup from a gushing spring is brought round for them, white, delicious to the drinkers, wherein there is no headache nor are they made mad [i.e., drunk] thereby. And with them are those of modest gaze, with lovely eyes, (pure) as they were hidden eggs (of the ostrich)" (Sura 37:40–49).

This vision is a repeated preoccupation of the Koran. Those who have won Allah's favor "shall recline on jeweled couches face to face, and there shall wait on them immortal youths with bowls and ewers and a cup of purest wine [that will neither pain their heads nor take away their reason]; with fruits of their own choice and flesh of fowls that they relish. And theirs shall be the dark-eyed houris, chaste as hidden pearls: a guerdon for their deeds" (Sura 56:15–24).

The *houris* are the legendary beautiful virgins who never lose their virginity, no matter how often they are ravished. Thus Paradise contains the earthly pleasures that Muslims are forbidden on earth: rich, abundant wine, all kinds of fruits and choice foods, and free sexual relations. Also present in this distinctly male-oriented Paradise are some of the pleasures of Sodom and Gomorrah: the "immortal youths" in the above passage from Sura 56 are not in Muslim tradition considered to be waiters only.

A Catholic would say this is a remarkably carnal and even boring Heaven. While it might be enjoyable for a week or even a month or year, this type of purely sensual paradise surely would prove unsatisfying for an eternity. Such a "heaven" would not satisfy the deepest longings of the human heart — namely, a greater union with and knowledge of our loving Creator. As Saint Augustine states in his *Confessions*: "Our hearts are restless unless they rest in Thee."

71. Do Muslim women experience the same type of Paradise as men?

The Koran does not say what the afterlife will be like for women. But Muhammad, meanwhile, does say that Hell will be filled with more women than men: "Once Allah's Apostle went out to the Musalla [to offer the prayer] of 'Id-al-Adha or Al-Fitr prayer. Then he passed by the women and said, 'O women! Give alms, as I have seen that the majority of the dwellers of Hell-fire were you [women]. . . . You curse frequently and are ungrateful to your husbands. I have not seen anyone more deficient in intelligence and religion than you. A cautious sensible man could be led astray by some of you."[69]

Also, as we have seen, the Hadith even contains hints that black Muslims do not enter this Paradise (see question 45). Muslims today would prefer to ignore such embarrassing elements of the Hadith, but they cannot expunge them.

From a Christian perspective, such an "eternal discrimination" against women (and other races) is entirely foreign to the teaching of Jesus. In Galatians 3:28, St. Paul enunciates the equality of all before God in the most eloquent terms: "There is neither Jew nor Greek, there is neither slave nor free person, there is not male or female; for you are all one in Christ Jesus." All those who are saved are, therefore, admitted into the presence of God irrespective of race, worldly status, or gender. Only our fidelity to the will of God — that is, how well we have responded to His grace — matters in the end.

72. What is Islam's view of the end times?

The Muslim vision of the end times is filled with bloodshed: "Allah's Apostle said, 'The Hour will not be established until you fight with the Jews, and the stone behind which a Jew will be hiding will say, 'O Muslim! There is a Jew hiding behind me, so kill him.' "[70] Another Hadith also strikes a chilling note: "When judgment day arrives, Allah will give every Muslim, a Jew or Christian to kill so that the Muslim will not enter into hell fire."[71]

Muslims in general hold to no single established sequence of eschatological events, but some traditions offer glimpses of a fully-realized eschatological theology that borrows heavily from Christianity. According to one Hadith, Muhammad painted an end times scenario that centers on the return of Jesus: "He will descend [to the earth]. When you see him, recognize him — a man of medium height, reddish fair, wearing two light yellow garments, looking as if drops were falling down from his head though it will not be wet. He will fight the people for the cause of Islam. He will break the cross, kill swine, and abolish jizya [the special tax on nun-Muslims in Muslim societies]. Allah will perish all religions except Islam. He will destroy the Antichrist and will live on the earth for forty years and then he will die. The Muslims will pray over him."[72]

73. Is it true that a Muslim man may have more than one wife?

Yes, a Muslim man can have up to four wives. In the Koran, Sura 4:3 states, "If you fear that you cannot treat orphans (orphan girls) with fairness, then you may marry other women who seem good to you: two, three, or four of them." This verse continues by offering a small hope for a woman who hopes to have an exclusive relationship with her husband: "But if you fear that you cannot maintain equality among them, marry one only or any slave-girls you may own."

Muslim monogamy advocates link this warning with the Koranic assertion that "try as you may, you cannot treat all your wives impartially" (Sura 4:129) to argue that since no man could treat his wives impartially, he should only marry one woman. Certainly in contemporary Islamic society there are many monogamous unions, but according to the word of the Koran (and how it is understood in most Muslim countries), a man always has the option to take several wives.

From a Catholic perspective, polygamy is antithetical to the essential nature of marriage: a lifetime covenant between a man and woman, a total self-giving rooted in and reflecting Jesus' covenant with His Church. In Christian marriage, the two spouses become one flesh, thereby entering into a life of sacrificial love. This type of covenant is by its very nature exclusive; it cannot admit others into its intimacy. A man cannot truly become "one flesh" with more than one living woman.

74. How many wives did Muhammad have?

Until he was forty years old, Muhammad had only one wife. This was Khadija, a businesswoman who was said to be fifteen years older than Muhammad and even to have been his employer before they married. As we have seen, when he first began to receive revelations of the Koran, Muhammad found comfort and reassurance from Khadija. But she died not long after he began to receive these revelations. Subsequently the Prophet embarked upon a series of marriages — as many as fourteen, although not all fourteen women were alive at the same time. He contracted many of these marriages for political reasons.[73]

Muhammad even married the ex-wife of his adopted son. It is said that Zaynab bint Jahsh possessed remarkable beauty; Muhammad chanced upon her not fully clothed and went away overcome. Zaid, his adopted son, offered to divorce her so that the Prophet could marry her. Muhammad told him to go back to his wife, but then Allah is said to have intervened, and He commanded Muhammad to marry Zaynab (see Sura 33:37). So Muhammad took Zaynab as his wife, protected by Allah's own words from the appearance of scandal.

Most notoriously, Muhammad married the nine-year-old Aisha. While this would be a scandal today, in Muhammad's time marriages with girls this young were not uncommon. The problem is that Muhammad's example makes it extremely difficult today to stamp out child marriage in the Islamic world.

Lest there be any whisperings about Muhammad's large number of wives, Allah gave him special permission to have more than the ordinary Muslim.[74]

75. What does the Koran teach about slavery?

The Koran assumes the existence of slavery. This appears particularly in marriage law, which allows a man to amass slave girls in addition to his four wives: "Forbidden to you are your mothers, your daughters, your sisters, your paternal and maternal aunts . . . Also married women, except those whom you own as slaves. Such is the decree of God" (Sura 4:23–24).

Islam was born in an era when slavery was taken for granted. A warrior acquired slave girls after every victorious battle. A man could gather as many slave-girls as he was able, in addition to his wives. Such behavior would be a relic of the past were it not for the fact that the Koran, by assuming the goodness of slavery in such passages, gives slavery the seal of Allah's words. Thus the only place in the world where slavery persists today is in Sudan and Mauritania, two Muslim countries, and there is evidence that its practice is more widespread than that. Amnesty International has found that Muslim Pakistan is "both a country of origin and a transit country for the trafficking of women for domestic labor, forced marriage and prostitution. This form of slavery is organized by crime networks that span South Asia. Some women, both local and trafficked, are killed if they refuse to earn money in prostitution."[75] Slavery also seems to be quietly tolerated today in other Muslim countries.

While the Bible was also written at a time when slavery was a fact of life, its teachings about the dignity of all human beings before God ultimately allowed anti-slavery forces to work for abolition under the banner of Christianity. This is much more difficult in Islam: what Allah says is applicable for all times, unless He Himself abrogates it. Also, the Koran nowhere teaches that all human beings have dignity before Allah. Its repeated and vociferous denunciation of unbelievers actually militates against this idea. It even portrays Jews and Christians as having been cursed by Allah and transformed into detested beasts, as evidenced by the notorious "apes and swine" verse quoted previously (see Sura 5:59–60).

76. How did Islam spread throughout the world? Where are the largest concentrations of Muslims today?

Islam has spread by the word and by the sword. Mass conversions to Islam followed the Muslim conquests of the Middle East, Egypt, and the rest of North Africa. Muslims also led incursion eastward from Arabia, conquering large portions of India and converting many Indians to Islam.

On the other hand, Islam spread by largely peaceful means into Malaysia and Indonesia, as well as large areas of sub-

Saharan Africa. In recent years, however, both of these areas have been flashpoints of violence between Muslims and non-Muslims.

Most of the conquests Muslim forces made were permanent. Only in Spain were they rolled back on a large scale, and that took a 700-year struggle. But most of the lands of North Africa and the Middle East, as well as the Arabian home of Islam, are virtually 100 percent Muslim today — although there are still significant (but rapidly dwindling) Christian minority communities in many of these countries, especially in Egypt, Syria, and Iraq. Christians long formed a majority in Lebanon, but now the situation in that war-torn nation is quite volatile. From the mid-1970s until the early 1990s a bloody civil war raged in Lebanon. Among its many sad effects has been a sharp increase in the number of Christians leaving the country. Muslims, meanwhile, have streamed into the country from the surrounding nations with the explicit ultimate goal of transforming what had once been envisioned by the United Nations as a Christian homeland in the Middle East into an Islamic state.

Outside of the Middle East, the non-Arab nations of Iran, Pakistan, Afghanistan, Uzbekistan, Turkmenistan, Kazakhstan, Kyrgyzstan, Azerbaijan, Bangladesh, and Indonesia are also predominantly Muslim. Malaysia and the Philippines have significant Muslim populations, and Islam is spreading quickly today out of its longtime North African base into sub-Saharan Africa.

Due to recent emigration, Muslims now also make up sizeable minorities in many European countries (particularly Germany, France, and England) and in North America as well. It is probable that the Muslim populations of all these traditionally non-Muslim areas will continue to grow for the foreseeable future.

77. Were Muslims ever persecuted in Christian countries?

Yes, there have been a few isolated instances of Muslim persecution at the hands of Christians. These instances, however, were directly related to the expansion of Islam (usually by the sword) into traditionally Christian regions. A few examples:

After the 700-year *reconquista* (the struggle of Spanish Christians to regain their homeland after its conquest by Islam), Muslims were expelled from Spain.

When Christian armies captured Jerusalem in 1099 during the First Crusade, they began a bloody orgy of killing, rape, and plunder that lasted for days and has become the paradigmatic image of the Crusader in the Muslim world. When Osama bin Laden and other terrorist Muslims call American forces "Crusaders," it is this image they are trying to invoke.

Other than these isolated occurrences, it is hard to find examples of large-scale mistreatment of Muslims by Christians. Because Muslim forces pressed for so long into Christian Europe, and the state of war continued for so long, few Muslims settled in those Christian nations until modern times — when they had become secular states, shorn of their specifically Christian character.

The treatment of Christians in Muslim lands is another story altogether. It begins with the Islamic theology of *jihad*.

78. What is *jihad*?

The literal meaning of jihad is "to struggle, to strive hard, and to fight." The first two meanings are often cited by Muslims today to prove that jihad refers only to the individual's interior struggle against sin. Muslim apologists like to point out that jihad does not mean "holy war." Yet in Islamic history and theology, jihad has most often meant precisely that: holy war.

Some fundamentalist Islamic sects add jihad as the sixth pillar of the faith, emphasizing that Muslims have a duty to fight against unbelievers or infidels. Jihad is not termed a pillar of the faith in either the Koran or Hadith, but it is a large preoccupation of both. This clear importance leads these radical Muslim sects to give it the status of a pillar of Islam.

79. Does Islam require all Muslims to join in a jihad against unbelievers?

There are a great deal of untruths and half-truths being purveyed about jihad today, but the Koran is clear. It contains numerous verses that state in no uncertain terms that *unless* a Muslim takes up arms against the infidels, he is not a true Muslim and has no part in the Paradise promised to Muslims.

The question is complicated by the fact that there are also many contradictory verses in the Koran. Some state that one is not a true Muslim if he shrinks back from fighting against and killing the unbelievers, but others say that Muslims should *not* fight non-Muslims. Compare the fury of Sura 9:5 ("Slay the idolaters wherever you find them") with the live-and-let-live attitude of Sura 109:1–6 ("Say, 'Unbelievers, I do not worship what you worship, nor do you worship what I worship. . . . You have your own religion, and I have mine").

The problem with the Koran is the same as with the Bible: people can take verses out of their proper context and use them to make any case they want to make. Both sides of the ongoing debate about what the Koran really teaches about jihad accuse the other of taking verses out of context.

The context is indeed the key to understanding why the Koran contains such contradictory commands about jihad. To understand fully the true Koranic usage of the word *jihad*, we must examine how Muhammad's strategy in dealing with those who rejected his message evolved during his lifetime. We also need to understand certain important developments in Islam after Muhammad's death, especially later attitudes toward non-believers, since they also seem to have found their way into the Koran. Finally, we must consider as well the sheer volume of verses in the Koran declaring that Muslims are duty-bound to fight until Islam has conquered and eradicated all of its earthly enemies.

One of the verses most quoted by Muslims in conversation with Christians is "There shall be no compulsion in religion" (Sura 2:256). Similar texts include Suras 3:20; 6:107; and 16:125. Most scholars believe that these verses date from the early period of Muhammad's prophetic career, when he still harbored the hope that Jews and Christians would freely accept his prophetic status.

Unfortunately, this relatively pacifist version of Islam, popular as it is among Western commentators, was superseded during Muhammad's lifetime. Later in the Prophet's career he turned furiously on the Jews and Christians who rejected him, and began to preach that they must be conquered by force. Accordingly, the overwhelming majority of Koranic texts insist that fighting the unbeliever is mandatory. The same Sura that proclaims that there is "no compulsion in religion" (Sura 2:256) also contains this unyielding directive: "Fight against them until idolatry is no more and Allah's religion reigns supreme. . ." (Sura 2:193). This command is repeated in the same open-ended form in Sura 8:39: "Make war on them until idolatry shall cease and Allah's religion shall reign supreme."

Within the context of the abrogation theory, because violent verses like those quoted above were revealed later than the more peaceful ones, the peaceful verses have been nullified. Although many Muslim scholars today like to quote the peaceful texts in public forums, these verses actually have very little standing in Islamic theology. The famous silence of moderate Muslim clerics after the September 11, 2001 terrorist attacks can be explained in part by the uncomfortable reality of the abrogation theory.

80. I have heard that the majority of Muslims believe jihad should be used only defensively, that is, to protect and strengthen Islam against danger and corruption. Is this correct?

Yes. Most Muslim theologians maintain that jihad must only be a defensive struggle, though what exactly constitutes a defensive struggle is also the subject of wide disagreement and furious debate. The argument centers mainly on one Koranic verse: "Fight for the sake of Allah those that fight against you, but do not attack them first. Allah does not love the aggressors. Slay them wherever you find them. Drive them out of the places from which they drove you. Idolatry is worse than carnage" (Sura 2:190–191).

Yet the Koran also contains more open-ended exhortations to jihad:

Fight against those who believe not in Allah nor the Last Day, nor hold that forbidden which has been forbidden by Allah and His Messenger, nor acknowledge the religion of truth, from among the People of the Book, until they pay the jizya [the special tax on non-Muslims] with willing submission, and feel themselves subdued (Sura 9:29).

The "People of the Book" to which the Koran refers are, of course, primarily Jews and Christians. On the basis of this verse and others, the influential Shafi'i school of Muslim jurisprudence rejects the idea that jihad should only be defensive. The Shafi'i school holds sway today at Al-Azhar University in Cairo, Egypt, the Islamic world's oldest, most respected institution of higher learning and the school of some of the greatest minds of Islamic theology. Other verses enjoin Muhammad to

> fight in Allah's cause . . . and rouse the believers. It may be that Allah will restrain the fury of the unbelievers. . . . They only wish that you would reject Faith, as they do, and thus be on the same footing as they. So do not take friends from their ranks until they flee in the way of Allah from what is forbidden. But if they turn renegades, seize them and slay them . . ." (Sura 4:84, 89; see also Suras 9:73 and 47:4).

There is also justification in the Hadith for the use of lethal force against nonbelievers.[76]

It is also crucial to realize that the interpretation of the Koran and Hadith is not undertaken only by Islamic theologians, but also by individual mullahs in local mosques. Therefore the scholarly or historical context of a verse is often of little importance; whatever a verse originally meant, its interpretation is subject to contemporary influences. Also, the interpretations are subject to the knowledge and mindset of the individual mullah and can involve his prejudices, his national culture, and other factors. Unfortunately, many times in history, the interpretation of the Koran by Islamic leaders has been used to incite violence against nonbelievers. When tribes and nations have been threatened from within, they have been able to whip up unity by turning the eyes of their followers to the more violent verses. This brings about a temporary unity, based on Islam, within tribes and nations. This unity has fostered a "crowd mentality," easily exploitable by Muslim rulers who can use the cause of jihad to take the minds of their subjects away from day-to-day concerns.

81. How have Muslims responded to this call to jihad over the centuries?

The name given in traditional Islamic theology for the non-Muslim world is the "house of war." The responsibility of the "house of Islam" is to make war on unbelievers until they convert to Islam, are killed, or submit to second-class status under Islamic rule. These three choices are based on Sura 9:29: "Fight those who believe not in Allah nor the Last Day, nor hold that forbidden which hath been forbidden by Allah and His Messenger, nor acknowledge the religion of Truth, [even if they are] of the People of the Book [that is, Jews and Christians], until they pay the Jizya with willing submission, and feel themselves subdued." The Prophet Muhammad himself elaborates these choices in a well-known Hadith.[77]

From the earliest days of Islam, Muslims have acted on these commands. First Muhammad unified the Arabian peninsula under his rule and directed that all religions be forbidden there except Islam. (This is why even today Saudi Arabia forbids all religions except Islam to be practiced on its soil.)

Then the Muslims turned to the larger non-Muslim world. Muslim Arabia was surrounded by predominantly Christian lands, particularly the Byzantine imperial holdings of Syria, Palestine, and Egypt. Four of Christendom's five principal cities — Constantinople, Alexandria, Antioch, and Jerusalem — lay within striking distance of Arabia. The Byzantine Empire's great rival, Persia, also had a significant Christian population.

Muhammad himself made the first Islamic overtures to these neighbors. He sent letters to the leaders of Persia, Byzantium, and Abyssinia, exhorting them to "embrace

Islam and you will be safe."[78] None did, and Muhammad's warning proved accurate: none of them were safe. In 635 (just three years after the Prophet's death), Damascus, the city where Paul had seen the great vision that turned him from a persecutor of Christianity to its energetic apostle, fell to the invading Muslims. The next year, Antioch, where the disciples of Jesus were first called "Christians" (Acts 11:26) also fell. It was Jerusalem's turn two years later, in 638.

Around the same time came the turn of Egypt, long a bastion of Christianity and home to great saints of the early Church such as St. Anthony of Egypt, St. Athanasius, and St. Cyril of Alexandria. Perhaps because there was so much resistance, the invaders were especially brutal. Many native Christians were killed; others were enslaved.[79] The same pattern prevailed when the Muslims reached Cilicia and Caesarea of Cappadocia in the year 650. In the same period, Muslim forces carried out raids on Cyprus, Rhodes, Crete, and Sicily, carrying off booty and thousands of slaves.[80]

These were mere preludes to the first great Muslim sieges of what was then the grandest city of Eastern Christendom and one of the greatest in the world: Constantinople. Muslim armies laid siege in 668 (and for several years thereafter) and again in 717. Both sieges failed, but they made it abundantly clear that the house of Islam had no intention of peacefully coexisting with Christendom.[81]

Did the motives for these initial conquests include a theological element? Without a doubt: this was the Muslim concept of jihad, or war against non-Muslims. One Muslim leader of that era put it this way: "The Great God says in the Koran: 'O true believers, when you encounter the unbelievers, strike off their heads.' The above command of the Great God is a great command and must be respected and followed."[82] He was referring to this verse of the Koran:

"When you meet the unbelievers in the battlefield, strike off their heads and, when you have laid them low, bind your captives firmly" (Sura 47:4).

Muslims rapidly swept through Christian North Africa, home of St. Cyprian of Carthage and St. Augustine of Hippo, and by 711 were in a position to invade Spain. Thus, Christian Europe was beset from both the East and the West. The campaign went well — so well, in fact, that the Muslim commander, Tarik, exceeded his orders and pressed his victorious army forward. When he was upbraided by the North African emir Musa and asked why he had gone so far into Christian Spain in defiance of orders, Tarik replied simply, "To serve Islam."[83]

He served Islam so well that, by 715, the Muslims were well on their way to conquering all of Spain (which they would hold for over 700 years), and they began pressing into France. Charles Martel (a name meaning "the Hammer"), grandfather of Charlemagne, stopped them at Tours in 732. Edward Gibbon, author of *The Decline and Fall of the Roman Empire*, observed that if the Muslim incursion into France had been successful, "perhaps the interpretation of the Koran would now be taught in the schools of Oxford and her pulpits might demonstrate to a circumcised people the sanctity and truth of the revelation of Mahomet."[84]

Despite this defeat, the Muslims did not give up. In 792, the ruler of Muslim Spain, Hisham, called for a new expedition into France. Muslims worldwide enthusiastically responded to his call to jihad, and the army that gathered was able to do a good deal of damage before it was ultimately defeated. France would remain a Christian country.

It is important to note that Hisham's call was religiously-based and that it preceded the Crusades (the supposed beginning of Christian-Muslim hostility) by more than three hundred years. Some fifty years later, in 848, France was again invaded by another Muslim army, a force that wreaked considerable havoc. Over time, however, Muslim fervor faded. In the course of the Muslim occupation, many of the occupiers were converted to Christianity, and the force dissipated.

Somewhat earlier, in 827, the warriors of jihad set their sights on Sicily and Italy. The commander of the invading force was a noted scholar of the Koran who forthrightly cast the expedition as a religious war. All through these lands they pillaged and looted Christian churches, terrorizing monks and violating nuns. By 846 they had reached Rome, where they exacted a promise of tribute from the Pope. While their hold on Italy was never strong, they held Sicily until 1091, when they were finally driven out by the Normans.

At the same time, Muslim armies continued to press Christendom's eastern flank. The Seljuk Turks decisively defeated the forces of the Byzantine Empire at the Armenian town of Moniker in 1071, paving the way for the Muslim occupation of virtually all of Asia Minor — some of the central and most well-known lands of Christendom. Henceforth Christians would be second-class citizens in the great Christian cities to which St. Paul addressed many of his canonical epistles: Ephesus, Colossae, and Philippi, as well as the region of Galatia.

While Crusades were mounted intermittently over the next two centuries, and though they had some initial success, they did little to stem the tide of jihad. Then in 1345, the Byzantine Emperor John VI, dynastic disputes having rendered him short-sighted, asked for help from the Turks to further his own cause. They arrived in Europe to help him – and decided to stay. On June 15, 1389, they engaged Christian forces in battle at a place that has fresher associations of horror in the modern mind: Kosovo. Once again, the battle was a religious one, for the strategizing on the

Muslim side had a strong theological flavor. On the night before the battle:

> The grand vizier opened the Koran at random seeking inspiration. His eyes fell upon the verse that said, "Oh Prophet, fight the hypocrites and unbelievers." "These Christian dogs are unbelievers and hypocrites," he said. "We fight them."[85]

Fight the Christians they did, and ultimately prevailed against a stronger, larger force — making June 15 a day of mourning for Serbs ever after. This battle inaugurated the religious and ethnic fissures of the Balkans that continue to plague that unhappy region to this day.

Seven years later, in 1396, the Muslims defeated a French force that had traveled across Europe to come to the aid of the Hungarians; but now Hungary lay within the grasp of the Sultan. At this point, however, the onslaught of jihad against Christendom was slowed by an internal matter: the Ottoman Sultan had to fight off the Mongols from the East, who by this time were also Muslims. This was only a temporary delay, however. In 1444 Muslim armies again won a great victory over Christian forces at Varna. Soon thereafter they were in a position to take one of the greatest prizes of all: Constantinople, the capital of the Eastern Roman Empire and the second See of Christendom, the home of what was then the grandest church in the world — the Cathedral of Holy Wisdom, or *Hagia Sophia*.

The siege of Constantinople went on for several months, as the defenders of the great city held out against incredible odds. But it was only a matter of time given the strength and size of the Muslim forces. During a procession around the city, a famous and treasured icon of the Mother of God fell to the ground, and it took five men to restore it to its position; many took this as a sign that divine favor was leaving the city. In any case, Constantinople fell on Tuesday, May 29, 1453. Greeks still consider Tuesdays bad luck.

The victorious warriors entered the Hagia Sophia, where the faithful had gathered to pray during the city's last agony. They interrupted the Liturgy — Greek legend has it that the priests took the sacred vessels and disappeared into the cathedral's eastern wall, from where they shall return to complete the Divine Liturgy when the building is a church again — and killed everyone they could. The Hagia Sophia became a mosque (today it is a museum, although Muslims — but not Christians — are still allowed to pray there). Hundreds of other churches suffered the same fate. But even then the advance was not over.

The Turks besieged Belgrade in 1456 and even tried to get to Rome, but at this point they were turned back. The tide was starting to turn. Europe, which had so long lagged behind the Islamic world, was catching up militarily. The Muslims were turned away from Malta in the sixteenth century, and failed in their first siege of Vienna in 1529. On October 6, 1571, the naval forces of the Holy Roman Empire won a decisive victory over the Ottoman navy at the great Battle of Lepanto. Later, though, a Muslim army defeated the Poles in 1672 and seized large portions of the Ukraine — but they lost what they had gained less than ten years later. Finally, they besieged Vienna again, only to be finally turned back on a day that marks the high point of Muslim expansion in Europe: September 11, 1683. (Osama bin Laden has never said so, but it seems likely that this date loomed large in his mind as he planned the attacks on the World Trade Center and the Pentagon.)

After the defeat at Vienna, the jihads vanished into historical memory. The European powers grew to be far stronger than the increasingly decrepit Ottoman Empire, until finally they were able to colonize larger portions of what had been Ottoman domains. The poverty and cultural and technological inferiority of the house of Islam made jihad impossible.

But the theology of jihad was set aside only in practice, not in theory. This theology has never been repudiated by any significant Muslim sect.

82. Doesn't the Bible (especially the Old Testament) contain violence similar to Islam's command for jihad?

Yes and no. The Old Testament contains a great deal of violence, much of it committed by men such as Joshua, who are depicted as heroes. However, the Jewish and Christian traditions long ago developed historical understandings of God's Word; this allowed them to see the principles embodied in the Old Testament's violent passages as applicable for one time and place but not universally. The only theological mechanism that approximates this for Muslims is, as we have seen, the abrogation theory, but this approach is actually used to support the Koran's violent passages.

Most importantly, there is not a single verse in the entire Bible that contains an open-ended, universal command to kill unbelievers. No Crusader could point to any words of Jesus as the justification for his taking up arms beyond oblique statements such as: "I have not come to bring peace, but a sword" (Mt 10:34). Most often in Christian tradition such statements have been understood in a spiritualized manner, that is, a believer's faith in Jesus will bring him or her into spiritual conflict with the world, the flesh, and the Devil. When read in its proper context, it is clear that Jesus is certainly not calling for violent struggle against non-Christians.

But in the Koran, as we have seen, there are many verses that command believers to fight unbelievers. Those who contend that they are to be understood only spiritually or as not applicable today face an uphill battle, for they are fighting against not only the plain words of the text but a large portion of Islamic tradition.

83. Weren't the Christian Crusades similar to the Islamic view of jihad?

No, they were not. The Crusades were a call from the Church to take back the lands overrun by Muslim invaders and, by extension, to free those Christians living under Islamic oppression.

Pope Urban II called the first Crusade in 1095. A mission to convert, kill, or subdue non-Christians does not seem to have formed any part of his conscious intentions. For Urban, this Crusade was a long overdue defensive action:

> For your brethren who live in the east are in urgent need of your help, and you must hasten to give them the aid which has often been promised them. For, as most of you have heard, the Turks and Arabs have attacked them and have conquered the territory of Romania [the Greek empire] as far west as the shore of the Mediterranean and the Hellespont, which is called the Arm of St. George. They have occupied more and more of the lands of those Christians, and have overcome them in seven battles. They have killed and captured many, and have destroyed the churches and devastated the empire. If you permit them to continue thus for awhile with impunity, the faithful of God will be much more widely attacked by them. On this account I, or rather the Lord, beseech you as Christ's heralds to publish this everywhere and to persuade all people of whatever rank, foot-soldiers and knights, poor and rich, to carry aid promptly to those Christians and to destroy that vile race from the lands of our friends.[86]

Note that the Pope says nothing about conversion or conquest: he only warns Christians that if they do not stand up to the Muslim armies, "the faithful of God will be much more widely attacked by them."

Certainly the motives of many Crusaders may not have been as pure as the Pope had intended, and this Crusade as well as the ones that followed foundered due to brutality and greed. But the idea that the Crusades were comparable to jihad in motive, or even predatory imperialist actions against a peaceful and indigenous Muslim population, is simply historically inaccurate. Such a view stems more from the prevailing Western sense of general guilt than from genuine historical research.

Modern commentators state that Islam had no hostile intentions toward the West until the advent of the Crusades, when Muslims had to defend themselves and their homes against predatory Christian invaders from the West. Combine that with the Islamic world's later humiliating experience with colonialism, say the pundits, add in the Israeli/Palestinian conflict, and you have in a nutshell the root causes of Osama bin Laden, the Ayatollah Khomeini, and the rest. All this is in service of the assumption that Islam is essentially a religion of peace, and that it was only Islamic mistreatment at the hands of Western non-Muslims (that is, Christians) that have made violent elements in Islam come to the fore. However, as we have seen, the facts of history are otherwise.

84. Are there different types of jihad?

Jihad has several meanings. Its application can cover almost every aspect of life. Islamic scholars divide jihad into two types: *greater jihad* and *lesser jihad*.

1. *Greater jihad* is the struggle of the individual Muslim to apply the tenets of Islam in daily life, and to live obediently and without sin. In other words, greater jihad stands for the constant inner moral struggle or constant reform of one's life.

2. *Lesser jihad* involves fighting the enemies of Allah in order to enhance Allah's dominion in the world. This fighting may not involve actual combat, but that is one of the

forms it can take. The theory of lesser jihad is not a product of the Koran or Hadith; it was actually formulated during the tenth through twelfth centuries, long after the death of Muhammad. However, its theological premises for taking up arms against unbelievers are drawn from the Koran.

Islamic theology specifies many forms of lesser jihad besides the taking up of arms. These are for both individuals and groups. They can be exercised by any individual Muslim or by social institutions under Muslim authority. Some of the forms of lesser jihad include the following: (1) *Migration to the infidels' lands for the sake of Muslim evangelization;* (2) *Oral jihad,* which is the apologetic struggle to defend Islam against detractors; (3) *Written jihad,* which involves publishing books, websites, and other forums to defend and spread Islam, or raising money and recruits for Islamic causes; (4) *Construction in jihad,* which involves building mosques and Islamic schools, especially in non-Muslim lands; (5) *Monetary support for jihad* (which involves establishing Islamic banks, insurance companies, trusts, and business partnerships; levying special taxes (*jizya*) on infidels; supporting the families of those who wage jihad in all its different forms [*the Mujahadeen*] — as well as the "martyrs" [*the Shaheed*] who have died in exercising lethal force or suicide attacks upon infidels); and (6) *Intelligence jihad,* which involves collecting information about Christian missionaries in Islamic countries via open public records of churches and organizations, and supplying these records to Islamic groups for the sake of countermeasures.

As you can see, the expansion of Islam is rooted in and supported by a well thought out system.

85. Since most of the world has not yet been converted to Islam, do Muslims still believe in universal jihad?

Yes. If Muslims take the Koran and Hadith seriously, they will fight until everyone on earth is Muslim, or at least until all are utterly subdued under Muslim rule. Muhammad's previously quoted words ("I have been ordered to fight with the people till they say, 'None has the right to be worshipped but Allah'") are open-ended and appear in numerous well-attested Hadiths.

However, not all Muslims today, of course, apply Muhammad's commands and Koranic principles to their lives. The Prophet himself predicted that only some of his followers would keep up the struggle: "A section of my community will continue to fight for the right and overcome their opponents till the last of them fights with the Antichrist."[87]

86. Given Islam's teachings on jihad, how can Muslims claim it is a religion of peace?

When the Muslim declares that Islam is a religion of peace, he is either ignorant of the Koran or is extending this "peace" only to those within the Muslim community, without telling you that is the way he means it. According to the Koran, "Muhammad is the Apostle of Allah. Those who follow him are merciful to one another, but ruthless to unbelievers" (Sura 48:29). Muslims are to greet and treat other fellow Muslims in a manner promoting peace within the *Umma*, or worldwide Muslim brotherhood. In Islam, there exists no true concept of peace between the nonbeliever and the devout Muslim. Peace can only exist for those who follow Islam.

87. Are suicide attacks by terrorists in the name of Islam justified by the Koran?

Opinions on this point differ among Muslim scholars. Some condemn suicide attacks on the basis of Sura 4:29: "O ye who believe! Eat not up your property among yourselves in vanities: But let there be amongst you traffic and trade by mutual good-will: Nor kill (or destroy) yourselves: for verily Allah hath been to you Most Merciful!"

However, other Muslim authorities justify suicide bombing, pointing out that numerous other verses promise Paradise to someone who is killed while fighting for Allah. Indeed, this is the only guarantee of Paradise given in the Koran:

> Therefore, when ye meet the Unbelievers (in fight), smite at their necks; At length, when ye have thoroughly subdued them, bind a bond firmly (on them) . . . But those who are slain in the way of Allah, He will never let their deeds be lost. Soon will He guide them and improve their condition, and admit them to the Garden which He has announced for them (Sura 47:4–6; see also Sura 3:157).

One passage chides those who shrink from fighting and praises those who wish for death:

> If a wound hath touched you, be sure a similar wound hath touched the others. Such days (of varying fortunes) We give to men and men by turns: that Allah may know those that believe, and that He may take to Himself from your ranks martyr-witnesses (to Truth). . . . Did ye think that ye would enter Heaven without Allah testing those of you who fought hard (In His Cause) and remained steadfast? Ye did indeed wish for death before ye met him: Now ye have seen him with your own eyes, (And ye flinch!) (Sura 3:140–143).

On the basis of these and other similar passages, the foremost cleric in Sunni Islam, Sheikh Muhammad Sayyid Tantawi, the Grand Sheikh of Al-Azhar University in Cairo, "emphasized that every martyrdom operation against any Israeli, including children, women, and teenagers, is a legitimate act according to [Islamic] religious law, and an Islamic commandment."[88] It seems clear that Tantawi's view is held by many in the Islamic world, judging from the events of recent history.

88. Why do many Muslims seem to hate the United States and the Western democracies?

There are several reasons for this. Muslims point to conflicts around the world where American forces, in attempting to resolve particular humanitarian or security issues, have seemed to oppose Muslims. A recent example of this was the Clinton Administration's mid-1990s military relief action in Somalia, a predominantly Muslim country. Some Muslims resent the continued American military presence in Saudi Arabia (dating from the 1991 Gulf War), as this is Islam's holy land. Muhammad clearly told his followers that only one religion — Islam — should ever be allowed there, but the vast majority of the American soldiers stationed in Saudi Arabia are non-Muslim. Their mere presence is offensive to many Muslims.

Others decry what they view as the immorality of Western secular societies and resent the West's technological superiority and cultural influence. If Islam is the final, perfect revelation, then many Muslims believe that Islamic society should also be preeminent in all facets of life. When Muslims see how far they are from this ideal, their resentment only grows.

In addition, because Muslims are called to support Islamic causes and fellow Muslims, they typically support the Palestinians in their conflict with Israel. In the Muslim world it is widely believed that the United States (and the West as a whole) is an uncritical supporter of Israel. Since the vast majority of Palestinians are Muslims, all Muslims are called to support them and, indeed, all causes that are perceived to be causes of Islam. It does not matter to most Muslims whether individual Americans support war with Muslim countries or not — all Americans are part of the West and, as such, are considered to be "crusaders" against Islam no matter what.

89. If it is a religion of peace, why does Islam impose the death penalty on Muslims who leave the faith?

Islam makes great use of fear to restrain its adherents and to influence the conversion of unbelievers. As the Koran states: "Anyone who, after accepting faith in Allah, utters Unbelief — except under compulsion, his heart remaining firm in Faith — but such as open their breast to Unbelief, on them is Wrath from Allah, and theirs will be a dreadful Penalty" (Sura 16:106). In this life that penalty is a sentence of death, whenever and wherever Muslims are able and willing to carry it out. According to one respected manual of Islamic law, someone who forsakes Islam "deserves to die."[89]

From the earliest days of Muhammad's career until today, the sword has spread Islam. Compare this reliance on the "fear of the sword" with the Christian understanding of the role of "fear" of God (not man) as a starting point toward growth and freedom. In Christianity, "fear of God" is understood as reverence for God and His commandments; it is not a "servile" or "cowering" kind of fear — it is one of the seven gifts of the Holy Spirit (see CCC 1831). In the Bible, we read of the hope and promise that as one grows in love of God and neighbor, human fear will be removed by love, and one will live in the peace that surpasses understanding: "Perfect love casts out all fear" (1 Jn 4:18).

Surprising as it may be to non-Muslims, many Muslims have no trouble accepting the conflicting concepts of Islam as a religion of peace yet one that mandates death for apostates. They assume that the truth of Islam is so obvious that only an obstinate person would refuse to accept it. One of the three unforgivable sins in Islam is apostasy. Therefore, it is the religious duty of Muslims to kill those who convert from Islam to another faith. To them the only real peace comes from defending the true religion of God: Islam.

Professor Anh Nga Longva of the University of Bergen in Norway visited Kuwait in 1997 to investigate the case of Husayn Ali Qambar, a convert to Christianity from Islam who had been sentenced to death for his conversion. In discussions with Kuwaitis, Longva found that "those who opposed [the death penalty for Qambar] based their position on the Koranic verse (2:257) that says 'no compulsion is there in religion'. But more often than not, the same verse was quoted in front of me to show that precisely because Islam is such a tolerant religion, there are no possible excuses for apostasy."[90]

90. What is the difference between the Christian and Muslim views of evangelization? Don't both seek to convert the world?

The Christian is called by Jesus to spread the good news of the Gospel: that God is a loving Creator who desires that all people come to a full knowledge of Him, to have a relationship of love with Him and with one's neighbor.

Christians are called to love all people, especially their enemies (Mt 5:44). No other religion makes "the loving of one's enemies" so essential. Jesus teaches that there is no genuine way to peace other than through forgiveness of, and love for, one's enemies. Any religion that, in its scriptures, defines peace as doing violence to its enemies is offering a false peace based on conformity. Christian peace is based on love, which is inclusive, not exclusive, and therefore extends to all genuine peace.

Consider the difference in the following two stories, the first from the Gospel of John and the second from the Hadith. In the Gospel narrative, we read about the woman caught committing adultery. Note Jesus' response:

> Then each went to his own house, while Jesus went to the Mount of Olives. But early in the morning He arrived again in the temple area, and all the people started coming to Him, and He sat down and taught them. Then the scribes and the Pharisees brought a woman who had been caught in adultery and made her stand in the middle. They said to Him, 'Teacher, this woman was caught in the very act of committing adultery. Now in the law, Moses commanded us to stone such women. So what do you say?' They said this to test Him, so that they could have some charge to bring against Him. Jesus bent down and began to write on the ground with His finger. But when they continued asking Him, He straightened up and said to them, 'Let the one among you who is without sin be the first to throw a stone at her.' Again He bent down and wrote on the ground. And in response, they went away one by one, beginning with the elders. So He was left alone with the woman before Him. Then Jesus straightened up and said to her, 'Woman, where are they? Has no one condemned you?' She replied, 'No one, sir.' Then Jesus said, 'Neither do I condemn you. Go, (and) from now on do not sin any more (Jn 7:53–8:11).

The following episode is from the Hadith. Note how Muhammad's actions are in sharp contrast with those of Jesus:

> There came to him [the Holy Prophet] a woman from Ghamid and said: Allah's Messenger, I have committed adultery, so purify me. He [the Holy Prophet] turned her away. On the fol-

lowing day she said: Allah's Messenger, Why do you turn me away? . . . By Allah, I have become pregnant. He said: Well, if you insist upon it, then go away until you give birth to [the child]. When she was delivered she came with the child [wrapped] in a rag and said: Here is the child whom I have given birth to. He said: Go away and suckle him until you wean him. When she had weaned him, she came to him [the Holy Prophet] with the child who was holding a piece of bread in his hand. She said: Allah's Apostle, here is he as I have weaned him and he eats food. He [the Holy Prophet] entrusted the child to one of the Muslims and then pronounced punishment. And she was put in a ditch up to her chest and he commanded people and they stoned her. Khalid b Walid came forward with a stone which he flung at her head and there spurted blood on the face of Khalid and so he abused her. Allah's Apostle heard his [Khalid's] curse that he had hurled upon her. Thereupon he [the Holy Prophet] said: Khalid, be gentle. By Him in Whose Hand is my life, she has made such a repentance that even if a wrongful tax-collector were to repent, he would have been forgiven. Then giving command regarding her, he prayed over her and she was buried.[91]

These examples sum up two radically different understandings of repentance. Jesus accepts the woman's repentance and she is not punished; Muhammad accepts the woman's repentance but she is punished nevertheless. This also encapsulates a core difference between the messages that Christian and Muslim evangelists are spreading around the world today: one is a message of genuine mercy and love, the other is at its core one of fear and punishment.

91. Is a Christian's life in danger if he or she preaches the Gospel in an Islamic country?

Yes. If a Christian missionary attempts any form of visible Christian evangelization in an Islamic state, he is signing his death sentence under Islamic law. Christians, Jews, and other "infidels" are not allowed to speak freely or openly about their own faith, let alone attempt to evangelize Muslims. The restrictions placed on Christians in Saudi Arabia are particularly harsh: Christians are not allowed to bring Bibles into the country, nor to wear crosses, build churches, or practice their religion in any way while on Saudi soil. This is because "the Prophet on his deathbed, gave three orders [including], 'Expel the *Al-Mushrikun* [polytheists, pagans, idolaters, and disbelievers in the Oneness of Allah, and His Messenger Muhammad] from the Arabian Peninsula.' "[92] In Saudi Arabia, Christians may carry a Bible or a prayer book only at risk of a long prison sentence, expulsion from the country, or even death.

Saudi Arabia is not the only Muslim country where such overt discrimination against non-Muslims occurs. Because the Koran says they are under Allah's curse, Christians are treated with contempt — and much worse — throughout the Islamic world. They have suffered large-scale persecution in Indonesia, Algeria, Pakistan, Bangladesh, and elsewhere. In Sudan, some Muslims kidnap Christians and sell them into slavery. In Egypt, the government pays for mosques to be built, but it does not finance the construction of churches — it even refuses Christians the necessary construction permits to build churches. Muslims everywhere who convert to Christianity live in peril of their lives. Nowhere in the Islamic world do Christians live entirely free from fear of Muslim radicals.

Missionaries in Islamic states must be very cautious and secretive about their activities. But they have met with some success. There are thousands of converts from Islam to Christianity in the Middle East and elsewhere in the Islamic world, yet most keep their conversions secret. Otherwise, their lives and those of their families would be in danger.

92. Is it true that Christians living in an Islamic state must pay a special tax?

Yes, the Koran speaks of the *jizya*, a special tax imposed on non-Muslims: "Fight those who believe not in Allah nor the Last Day, nor hold that forbidden which hath been forbidden by Allah and His Messenger, nor acknowledge the religion of Truth, [even if they are] of the People of the Book, until they pay the jizya with willing submission, and feel themselves subdued" (Sura 9:29). According to Islamic law, the jizya is required from People of the Book (that is, Jews and Christians); laws governing its collection have sometimes been applied to all non-Muslims. Christians have to pay for their own protection and pay extra taxes on their property. These taxes apply only to Christians. No such tax applies to Muslims.

The fact that Christians have to pay for their protection in Islamic states is tantamount to extortion. Islamic theology categorizes Christians living in Islamic states as *Ahl Al-Dhimmi*: people under Islamic security or special protection. If one does not pay, he has no protection. The word *dhimmi* derives from *dhema*, which means "blamed, dispraised, or censured."

The second tax that Christians must pay according to Islamic law is the property tax. Some Islamic states do not enforce these taxes, but they are nevertheless on the books in case they are needed to bring some charge against a particular Christian. Western civil law guarantees equal treatment to all citizens, but the *Sharia*, or Islamic law, is firmly based on the superiority and preeminence of the Muslim community.

Islamic law adds other restrictions besides the tax. These laws can be found in a manual of the Sharia that, according to authorities at the respected Al-Azhar University, "conforms to the practice and faith of the orthodox Sunni Community."[93] It stipulates that non-Muslims in Muslim lands, particularly Jews and Christians, must wear dress that is distinct from that of Muslims, including a "wide cloth belt." They must not be given the Muslim greeting, *"As-Salamu 'alaykum"* ("Peace be with you"). They must "keep to the side of the street" — that is, step off a sidewalk to allow a Muslim to pass. They "may not build higher than or as high as the Muslims' buildings, though, if they acquire a tall house, it is not razed."

Jewish and Christian *dhimmis* also "are forbidden to openly display wine or pork . . . [another legal authority adds] to ring church bells or display crosses, recite the Torah or Evangel aloud, or make public display of their funerals and feast days." Perhaps most significantly, Christians "are forbidden to build new churches."[94]

If *dhimmis* do not follow these laws, their property and possibly their lives are forfeit.

Widely enforced in the Middle Ages and into the nineteenth century (and in some countries, notably Yemen, well into the twentieth), these laws fell by the wayside when much of the Islamic world was colonized by Western powers. Few Muslim countries enforce these laws today, but they are still officially part of the Sharia and thus can be brought to play again by any Muslim reformer who calls for a return to Islamic purity and the fullness of observance of the faith.

In various places Muslim authorities also restrict Christians and Jews from public proclamations of their faith. Christians are also forbidden to evangelize; they are forbidden to enter mosques. Thus no Christian preacher may ever enter a mosque and engage those within in religious debate (the way St. Paul entered synagogues to proclaim the Gospel). Though Pope John Paul II's visit to the Omayyad mosque in Damascus, Syria, in May of 2001 was certainly a bold (and fruitful) action, it seems to have been allowed only because he was not there to preach — he was there to "reach out" to Islam, to "build bridges of understanding" between Christians and Muslims.

Non-Islamic publications are tolerated in some places, but they often must be under the control of a department of the civil government that enforces Islamic laws and regulations in society. Finally, if a Muslim and a Christian wish to marry, the Christian must publicly accept Islam; otherwise the couple will incur civil and religious penalties.

93. How do the Catholic and Muslim views of justice differ?

There are some similarities in our respective views of justice, but also many differences. To begin with, the *premises* of justice in the two faiths are different, and thus the practical *implications* are often dramatically different.

The Islamic view of justice is based on Islamic theology, which regulates all aspects of life and codifies some laws that are unjust according to Catholic view of justice. For example, the testimony of a non-Muslim is not valued as highly as that of a Muslim, and a woman's testimony is devalued and inadmissible in certain cases. Draconian penalties, including stoning for adultery and amputation for theft, very much abound in Islam.

The Catholic view of justice, on the other hand, is rooted in the natural law. It is an expression of the God-given rights inherent in all human beings, regardless of nationality, religion, race, or gender. For a Catholic, justice means simply "to give another his due," that is, to recognize that the other person is endowed with the same natural rights and treat him or her accordingly (see CCC 1928). As the *Catechism of the Catholic Church* states, "Respect for the human person entails respect for the rights that flow from his dignity as a creature" (CCC 1930).

The core of these differences is the fact that Islam has never been eager to grant unbelievers, the "vilest of creatures" (Sura 98:6) — status equal to that of Muslims. Islam's radically different view of justice and human rights may also explain why many Muslim countries are noticeably underdeveloped in comparison with the West.[95] There are some exceptions to this (most notably, Turkey), but the fact remains — theology affects culture. This can be seen in Islam's denial of rights to non-Muslims, its acceptance of slavery, and its view of women as second-class citizens.

The Western notion that "all men are created equal" does not find much place in traditional Islamic thought and practice. According to Muslim journalist Amir Taheri, Sa'id Raja'i-Khorassani, the Permanent Delegate to the United Nations from Iran, said that "the very concept of human rights was 'a Judeo-Christian invention' and inadmissible in Islam. . . . According to Ayatollah Khomeini, one of the Shah's 'most despicable sins' was the fact that Iran was one of the original group of nations that drafted and approved the Universal Declaration of Human Rights."[96]

Taheri goes on to say that Islam "divides human beings into two groups: the Muslims and the non-Muslims. All male Muslims are equal and enjoy the same individual and collective rights and privileges. Non-Muslims living in a society where Muslims form the majority and control the state, however, are treated separately."[97]

94. What is the position of women in Islamic society? Do they have the same rights as men?

It is interesting to note that Muhammad seems to have actually improved the status of women compared to the polytheistic culture of his time. In pre-Islamic Arabia, female infants were often buried alive, a practice that the Koran would come to strongly condemn.[98] The ancient Arabs considered women as having no rights to inheritance; they were considered property; men could inherit a woman and all that she owned; and women could be forced into prostitution. The Koran condemned all of these practices and enjoined justice in inheritance rights (see Suras 4:7; 4:19; 24:33).

While these teachings of the Koran may have been revolutionary in seventh-century Arabia and may have corrected the most inhumane practices toward women and children, Islam has not progressed much further in its treatment of women.

Some Muslims, however, attempt to make Islam's teaching about women acceptable to modern sensibilities by claiming that the Koran teaches the equality of the sexes: "Men, have fear of your Lord, who created you from a single soul. From that soul He created its mate, and through them He bestrewed the earth with countless men and women" (Sura 4:1).[99] Similarly, Allah adds that "I will deny no man or woman among you the reward of their labours. You are the offspring of one another" (Sura 3:195).

There are a number of elements of the Koran's teaching about women that probably raised no eyebrows when originally formulated yet which are disquieting in a modern-day context. The treatment of women in Islamic countries is consistently shocking to modern Westerners. A notorious example of this occurred in the Muslim holy city of Mecca in March 2002, when fifteen girls perished in a school fire. The Saudi Arabian religious police, the *muttawa*, would not let the girls out of the building: in the female-only school environment, they had shed the all-concealing outer garments that Saudi women must wear in the presence of men. Since Saudi Arabia is one of the most fanatical and rigid Muslim countries, the *muttawa* preferred that the girls die rather than transgress Islamic law, and they actually battled police and firemen who were trying to open the school's doors.[100] This tragedy was a direct consequence of the way Islam's fundamental teachings and laws regard women.

The Koran teaches male superiority forthrightly: "Women shall with justice have rights similar to those exercised against them, although men have a status above women" (Sura 2:228). Also, "Men have authority over women because Allah has made the one superior to the other, and because they spend their wealth to maintain them" (Sura 4:34). Thus, Islam views women as innately subordinate to men; Allah made them that way. It's not hard to see, then, why women are treated as "second-class citizens" in traditional Muslim countries.

95. The Koran's teachings on the status of women seem to reflect those of St. Paul in the Bible. Didn't he tell wives to be submissive to their husbands?

St. Paul's teaching for wives to be submissive to their husbands must be read in the entire context of his letter to the Ephesians; indeed, it must be understood in the context of his epistles as a whole, and in light of the Gospels. Immediately prior to his "wives be submissive" injunction, St. Paul tells husbands and wives to "be subordinate [or submissive] *to one another* out of reverence for Christ" (Eph 5:21; emphasis added). Thus, in Christian theology, there is a mutual submission of husbands and wives to each another in love, a submission reflecting the Church's submission to Christ (see Eph 5:24). In fact, rather than exalting the authority of men over women, St. Paul goes on to place an even greater burden on men when he says "Husbands, love your wives, *even as Christ loved the Church and handed himself over for her* . . ."

(Eph 5:25; emphasis added). In other words, husbands must give their very lives to their spouses — they must sacrifice themselves and their own wills for the good of their wives and families.

The Koran, on the other hand, has a very different view of the relationship that exists between spouses. Husbands, by divine right, have total authority over their wives. In sharp contrast to St. Paul's teachings, the idea that a husband should sacrifice himself or live "in mutual submission" with his wife is entirely foreign to Islam. In fact, the same verse in the Koran that begins by stating that "men have authority over women" goes on to give divine sanction to wife-beating: "Good women are obedient. They guard their unseen parts because God has guarded them. As for those from whom you fear disobedience, admonish them and send them to beds apart and beat them" (Sura 4:34).

In Islam, the idea that "men have a status above women" is deeply rooted in Muslim tradition. Aisha, the most beloved of Muhammad's many wives, admonished women in no uncertain terms: "O womenfolk, if you knew the rights that your husbands have over you, every one of you would wipe the dust from her husband's feet with her face."[101]

Other disquieting elements of Islamic teaching about women and their rights include the inequality in receiving inheritance (men receive twice as much as women; see Sura 4:11) and the various laws regarding divorce.

96. What does Islam teach about divorce?

If a Muslim man is unhappy with any of his wives, he is free to divorce them by simply saying, "I divorce you." The Koran stipulates only that a man wait for a suitable interval in order to make sure that his wife is not pregnant (see Sura 65:1). If the divorcing couple has any children, they ordinarily go to live with their father.

In Islam, divorce can even be brought about by a third party. Nawal El-Saadawi, the feminist defender of Islamic tradition cited above, almost fell victim to this when a radical Muslim advocate brought suit to have her forcibly divorced from her husband on the grounds that she had apostatized (that is, formally left the faith). Presumably this judgment was based on her pointing out that Muslim veneration of the black stone of the Ka'aba, the center of the pilgrimage to Mecca, was a holdover from pre-Islamic paganism. Under heavy international pressure, an Egyptian court threw the case out in the summer of 2001.[102]

Since men can obtain divorces so easily, they often divorce capriciously. But The Koran offers some reprieve from this oppressive law: "If a man divorces his wife, he cannot re-marry her until she has wedded another man and been divorced by him" (Sura 2:230).

Rooted in Islam's liberal teachings on divorce is the phenomenon of the "temporary husband." After a husband has divorced his wife in a fit of anger, these men will "marry" the hapless divorcee for one night in order to allow her to return to her husband and family.

The apparent harshness of all this seems to be mitigated by another verse from the Koran: "If a woman fears ill-treatment or desertion on the part of her husband, it shall be no offense for them to seek a mutual agreement, for agreement is best" (Sura 4:128). But this call for an agreement is not a call for a meeting of equals — at least as it has been interpreted in the Hadith. Muhammad's wife Aisha has given an influential analysis of this verse: "It concerns the woman whose husband does not want to keep her with him any longer, but wants to divorce her and marry some other lady, so she says to him: 'Keep me and do not divorce me, and then marry another woman, and you may neither spend on me, nor sleep with me.' "[103]

The simplicity of divorce in Islam mirrors that of the Old Testament. In Deuteronomy 24:1–4, Moses teaches that a man may divorce his wife simply by writing her a "bill of divorce" and "dismiss her from his house." (Divorce was, of course, a one-way street — husbands could divorce their wives, but wives could not divorce their husbands.) In the New Testament, though, Jesus puts this teaching in context by saying God did not intend for divorce to occur, but Moses permitted it due to "the hardness of your hearts" (see Mt 19:8–9). He goes on to quote Genesis ("the two shall become one flesh"), indicating that marriage is by its very nature an indissoluble and permanent union.

97. Is it true that the testimony of a woman in court does not carry the same weight as that of a man?

Yes, and this unjust practice can have dramatic effects. One of these effects is the situation of rape as it plays out in conjunction with Islamic restrictions on the validity of a woman's witness. In court, a woman's testimony is worth half as much as that of a man. Says the Koran: "Call in two male witnesses from among you, but if two men cannot be found, then one man and two women whom you judge fit to act as witnesses; so that if either of them commit an error, the other will remember" (Sura 2:282).

Islamic legal theorists have restricted the validity of a woman's testimony even further by limiting it to, in the words of one Muslim legal manual, "cases involving property, or transactions dealing with property, such as sales."[104] Otherwise only men can testify. And in cases of sexual misbehavior, four male witnesses are required. They must not merely be witnesses who can testify that an instance of fornication, adultery, or rape happened: these witnesses must have seen the act itself.

This peculiar and destructive stipulation had its genesis in an incident in Muhammad's life: his wife, Aisha, was accused of infidelity. The accusation particularly distressed Muhammad because Aisha was his favorite wife. But in this case as in many others, Allah is said to have come to the aid of His Prophet: He revealed Aisha's innocence and instituted the stipulation of four witnesses for sexual sins: "Why did they not produce four witnesses? If they could not produce any witnesses, then they were surely lying in the sight of God" (Sura 24:13).[105]

Some Muslim authorities continue to insist that four male witnesses who saw the act itself must testify in any case involving sexual sin. *'Umdat al-Salik*, a classic manual of Islamic law that has been translated into English as *Reliance of the Traveller*, dictates that "if testimony concerns fornication or sodomy, then it requires four male witnesses."[106] According to Al-Azhar University, *Reliance of the Traveller* "conforms to the practice and faith of the orthodox Sunni Community."[107] Consequently, it is almost impossible to prove rape in lands that follow this understanding of Islamic law, the Sharia. If the required male witnesses cannot be found, the victim's charge of rape becomes an admission of adultery. This accounts for the grim fact that as many as 75 percent of the women in prison in Pakistan are behind bars for the "crime" of being a rape victim.[108]

This grim scenario played out recently in Nigeria. Two Muslim women, Sufiyatu Huseini and Amina Lawal, who stated but could not prove they were raped, were given the death sentence for adultery. Fortunately, neither sentence was carried out after rights groups worldwide brought

tremendous pressure upon Nigeria's Sharia court. Before
Huseini's sentence was revoked, however, it threw into sharp
relief the differences between Christianity and Islam. On
one hand, Aliyu Abubakar Sanyinna, the attorney general
of Nigeria's Sokoto state, defended the sentence: "It is the
law of Allah. By executing anybody that is convicted under
Islamic law, we are just complying with the laws of Allah,
so we don't have anything to worry about."[109] On the other
hand, the Archbishop of Lagos, Anthony Olubunmi Oko-
gie, offered to be stoned to death in Huseini's place.

98. Why do observant Muslim women wear full-covering clothing?

Muslim women who go outside their houses must be covered in order to show that they are believers, guarding their
modesty and displaying their beauty only to their husbands:
"O Prophet! Tell thy wives and daughters, and the believing women, that they should cast their outer garments over
their persons (when abroad): that is most convenient, that
they should be known (as such) and not molested" (Sura
33:59).

They should cast these outer garments over their entire
person: "Asma, daughter of Abu Bakr, entered upon the
Apostle of Allah wearing thin clothes. The Apostle of Allah
turned his attention from her. He said: 'O Asma, when a
woman reaches the age of menstruation, it does not suit her
that she displays her parts of body except this and this, and
he pointed to her face and hands.' "[110] While full-body cov-
ering was never required of Christian women, it is only recently that Christian society has lost all respect for the virtue
of female (and, for that matter, male) modesty in dress.

99. **It seems as if many Muslim countries are theocracies —
that is, religious leaders control political affairs. Is this
true?**

Yes and no. In one sense, this is less true today than it was
at many points in Islamic history. At the present time, religious leaders maintain a shaky grip on power in Iran, and
elsewhere in the Muslim world most countries are secular
states with little or no adherence to classic Islamic law, the
Sharia. These would include Turkey, Egypt, Syria, and Iraq
(during the rule of Saddam Hussein). Other states, notably
Saudi Arabia and Pakistan, follow the Sharia but are not
ruled by religious leaders as such; nonetheless, their laws
greatly discriminate against non-Muslims.

It is important to remember that Muhammad was a political and military leader as well as a religious one. As a result, politics and religion were more essentially intertwined
in Islam than in Christianity. From the beginning, Islam
has presented itself as a total way of life: a political and
social system as well as a religious faith. Many Muslims today press for the full enforcement of Islamic law in their
countries simply as an aspect of their fidelity to Islam.

100. **Should Muslims be evangelized by Christians or be left
alone?**

Some say that Christians should not speak to Muslims
about our faith, both because it is useless (even impossible)
to do so and because Muslims have their own covenant with
God. These notions are false and misguided for several reasons.

As for the idea that converting Muslims is impossible, our
Lord says that "with God, all things are possible" (Mt 19:26).
Christianity teaches that God wills for everyone to be saved

and come to the knowledge of the Truth, Jesus Christ, who came to preach the Gospel to all people without exception. In the Great Commission, Jesus commands His disciples to announce the Gospel to "all nations," going into the entire world (Mt 28:20). Throughout its history the Church has taken this call of Jesus seriously. Many Christians today, though, act as if Muslims are the exception to this command, and they complain about how hard it is to lead Muslims to Christ. Yet success is possible: in recent years many Muslims have embraced Christianity.

The evangelization of Muslims is not an unimportant issue. Nowadays many people tend to think that all religions are basically the same and that an individual's particular beliefs do not matter. They point out that both good and evil people can be found among all sects and creeds. While this is undeniably true (see Mt 7:21–23), it is beside the point: insufficient attention is given to the fact that not all religions expect the same things of people or call them to uphold the same standards. The command to "love your enemies" (Mt 5:44) is a higher, better call than the exhortation to be "merciless to unbelievers" (Sura 48:29). However well or poorly Christians live up to these words, they still stand as a microcosm of the mystery of Christ's Cross and the secret of peace for anyone who has the courage to live them out. Muslims should not be deprived of an opportunity to learn about the words and works of Jesus (and His revelation of God as Father) due to Christian indifference.

At the same time, some Christians advocate making common cause with Muslims on certain moral issues — fighting together for pro-life causes, for example. The Catholic Church has demonstrated the possibilities of such endeavors on a worldwide scale by joining with Muslim countries at the United Nations to defeat anti-life and anti-family initiatives. In light of such successes, it would be foolish to say that mutual cooperation between Christians and Muslims cannot happen.

However, in light of the elements of Islamic theology previously discussed, it is clear that such collaborations have their limits: some Muslims will never want to deal with Christians as equal partners. Their receptiveness to such initiatives will vary from place to place and issue to issue. This does not mean that Christians should not approach local Muslim groups to try to enlist their support on a particular issue about which Christians and Muslims agree, but they should be prepared for the possibility they may be rejected.

Regardless of whether our efforts are accepted or rejected, the urgency of our mission to Islam can be taken from the very words of Jesus Himself. There are three key New Testament passages that should inspire us in our efforts to evangelize Muslims:

1. In describing Himself as the Good Shepherd, Jesus tells his followers that "I came so that they might have life and have it more abundantly" (Jn 10:10). We must earnestly desire to bring this abundant life of Christ to Muslims and, indeed, to all who do not yet possess it.

2. In John 14:6, Jesus teaches: "I am the Way, the Truth, and the Life. No one come to the Father except through Me." We must strive to present the true Way, Truth, and Life to Muslims so that they might come to know God as their loving Father.

3. Immediately before His ascension into heaven, Jesus gives His disciples the Great Commission to preach His saving Gospel to all: "Make disciples of all nations, baptizing them in the name of the Father, and of the Son, and of the Holy Spirit, teaching them to observe all that I have commanded you" (Mt 28:19–20). This commission is ours as well.

Sharing the Gospel with Muslims

St. Francis of Assisi's advice to his own friars is a good place to start. He said: "Preach the Gospel with all your might; and if necessary, use words." Successful evangelization of others is mostly a witness to the treasure we hold in "earthen vessels" (see 2 Cor 4:7). Thus we have to prepare ourselves inwardly to bear witness to the Christian life outwardly. Daily living for God, consciously and continually choosing to live for God, and rejecting evil in all its forms is the necessary foundation for any successful evangelization effort.

Study what the Church actually teaches, so as to "be ready with an answer to those who ask you what is the cause of your joy" (1 Pt 3:15). Frequent the Sacraments, pray a great deal, and read and study the Scriptures and the writings of the Church Fathers. Digest the wisdom of the Scriptures and the light that the Fathers bring to them, until you intimately know the riches they contain. If you have an active spiritual life, you will have much to share with non-Christians about the power of the Resurrected Christ in your life.

Seek out personal relationships with Muslims, and strive to be as good a person as the person with whom you are speaking. Human nature is the same everywhere — the one true God created all human beings, and He is love. Whatever the official tenets of their faith, Muslims are just as likely to be kind and loving as anyone else.

Learn enough about Islamic theology to be able to recognize insincere or incomplete statements of Muslim belief. (You have taken a bold step in this direction by reading this book.) Much of what you bring up will be disputed immediately if it casts the Koran, Muhammad, or Allah in a bad light. Realize that much of what you may receive in return is distorted information, although the Muslim will be sincerely offering a defense of his faith.

Share a deeper understanding of what the Incarnation means and why this is not blasphemy, but rather is in accord with belief in a loving Creator. Explain how God wants a mutual relationship of love with His creatures, and how it would be contrary to His nature to be a "slave master." Focus on Jesus and His miracles as proof of that He was (and is) the Messiah, the Son of God. Explain how he could not be merely a prophet — He claimed to be "the Way, the Truth, and the Life" and clearly stated that "no one comes to the Father *but through Me*" (Jn 14:6).

Be prepared: the Muslims you meet may not even believe what we have told you in this book. Not many Muslims are well versed in their faith, and many, particularly in the United States, have been influenced by Western secular ideas. Many have not even read the Koran since they may not read Arabic, and yet they may still believe that only the Arabic Koran is the true Koran. They may know only the "spoken version" of Islam, which is subject to varying cultural influences and may or may not include all of the major doctrines of the faith.

It is wise not to assume that a particular Muslim believes all that we have discussed in this book, since our answers rely upon the sources of the faith: the Koran and the Hadith. The average Muslim may never examine these sources. If you ask your Muslim friend questions, you will quickly discover whether or not he has read the Koran and Hadith.

A good question to ask yourself is this: "Do I have as much zeal for the truth of Christ as the devout Muslim does for Islam?" But be forewarned! If you devote yourself to bringing the Gospel to Muslims, they will not see you as a fellow pilgrim moving toward the Kingdom or as a living temple of the Holy Spirit. To a serious Muslim, you will more likely be seen as an infidel with no real dignity or rights. You will be seen as a proper target of disinformation — half-truths and distortions of Islam designed to disarm and distract you from seeing the truth about the religion. Any good you do or evil you endure will be dismissed and your Christian virtue overlooked, since you will be regarded as an infidel and predestined by Allah for destruction in Hell. Some will even believe that they will be rewarded in Heaven for harming you or undermining your life.

What should the Christian reaction be to all of this? Ultimately, Christianity's unique and most compelling answer to Islam is the sacrificial love of Christ on the Cross. There is an immense difference between a life lived in the mistaken belief that the cross is a defeat and a humiliation (as Islam teaches) and a life lived in the profound truth that the Cross is man's only real source of victory and a liberation.

Insofar as we Christians are willing to imitate the sacrificial love of Christ, we will show Muslims the elements of mercy, compassion, and true peace that their religion is lacking. We will show them why, despite the tremendous obstacles, it is worthwhile to give everything for Jesus Christ. Insofar as we do not model this sacrificial love, of course, neither Muslims nor anyone else will see why they should prefer the Christian faith to their own.

This is our great challenge and our great responsibility.

Contradictory Teachings

Contradictory Teachings and Commands of Islamic Theology found in the Koran and Hadith

(Caution: this list is for your own information and reference. Do not present these points to Muslims without carefully reading Questions 47–49.)

Pharaoh repented and worshipped Allah: *"We took the Children of Israel across the sea: Pharaoh and his hosts followed them in insolence and spite. At length, when overwhelmed with the flood, he said: 'I believe that there is no god except Him Whom the Children of Israel believe in: I am of those who submit (to Allah in Islam).' (It was said to him): 'Ah now! But a little while before, wast thou in rebellion! And thou didst mischief (and violence)!*

This day shall We save thee in the body, that thou mayest be a sign to those who come after thee! but verily, many among mankind are heedless of Our Signs!'" (Sura 10:89–92).

Pharaoh did not repent and he was drowned: *"Moses said, 'Thou knowest well that these things have been sent down by none but the Lord of the heavens and the earth as eye-opening evidence: and I consider thee indeed, O Pharaoh, to be one doomed to destruction!' So he resolved to remove them from the face of the earth: but We did drown him and all who were with him"* (Sura 17:102–103).

No one is guilty of anyone else's sin: *"Every soul draws the meed of its acts on none but itself: no bearer of burdens can bear the burden of another"* (Sura 6:164).

Muhammad should forgive: *"We created not the heavens and the earth and all that is between them save with truth, and lo! the Hour is surely coming. So forgive, (O Muhammad), with a gracious forgiveness"* (Sura 15:85).

Prophets come only from the house of Israel. Referring to Abraham, the Koran says: *"And We bestowed on him Isaac and Jacob, and We established the prophethood and the Scripture among his seed, and We gave him his reward in the world, and lo! in the Hereafter he verily is among the righteous"* (Sura 29:27; see also Sura 45:16).

Allah accepts no intercession: *"Allah it is Who created the heavens and the earth, and that which is between them, in six Days. Then He mounted the Throne. Ye have not, beside Him, a protecting friend or mediator. Will ye not then remember?"* (Sura 32:4). *"Unto Allah belongs all intercession. His is the Sovereignty of the Heavens and the earth. And afterward unto Him ye will be brought back"* (Sura 39:44).

Cain is guilty of every drop of blood on earth: *"Whenever a person is murdered unjustly, there is a share of the burden of that crime on the first son of Adam, for he [Cain] was the first to start the tradition of murdering"* (Bukhari, vol. 4, book 60, no. 3335).

Muhammad should not forgive: *"O Prophet! Strive against the disbelievers and the hypocrites! Be harsh with them. Their ultimate abode is Hell, a hapless journey's end"* (Sura 9:73).

Ishmael is said to have been an Arab prophet before Muhammad: *"And make mention in the Scripture of Ishmael. Lo! he was a keeper of his promise, and he was a messenger (of Allah), a prophet"* (Sura 19:54).

Allah grants some permission for intercession: *"Lo! Your Lord is Allah Who created the heavens and the earth in six Days, and then He established Himself upon the Throne, directing all things. There is no intercessor save after His permission. That is Allah, your Lord, so worship Him. Oh, will ye not remind?"* (Sura 10:3).

Allah created the universe in eight days: *"Say: Is it that ye deny Him Who created the earth in two Days? And do ye join equals with Him? He is the Lord of (all) the Worlds. He set on the (earth), mountains standing firm, high above it, and bestowed blessings on the earth, and measure therein all things to give them nourishment in due proportion, in four Days, in accordance with (the needs of) those who seek (Sustenance). Moreover He comprehended in His design the sky, and it had been (as) smoke: He said to it and to the earth: 'Come ye together, willingly or unwillingly.' They said: 'We do come (together), in willing obedience.' So He completed them as seven firmaments in two Days, and He assigned to each heaven its duty and command. And We adorned the lower heaven with lights, and (provided it) with guard. Such is the Decree of (Him) the Exalted in Might, Full of Knowledge"* (Sura 41:9–12). Two days plus four days plus two days equal eight days.

Allah created the universe in six days: *"Your Guardian-Lord is Allah, Who created the heavens and the earth in six days, and is firmly established on the throne (of authority): He draweth the night as a veil o'er the day, each seeking the other in rapid succession: He created the sun, the moon, and the stars, (all) governed by laws under His command. Is it not His to create and to govern? Blessed be Allah, the Cherisher and Sustainer of the worlds!"* (Sura 7:54; see also Suras 10:3, 11:7, and 50:38).

The Koran states in many texts that its contents are easy to understand (Sura 44:58) and fully explained (Sura 6:114), that it contains detailed explanations of everything (Sura 12:111) and clear ordinance (Suras 16:89; 93:3). It was conveyed clearly (Sura 5:16, 10:15).

Some verses of the Koran are direct, but others are allegorical (Sura 3:7); it contains all matters of Similitude (Suras 18:54; 39:24). One should not approach it in haste (Sura 20:114). Its essence is found in the previous revelations (Sura 26:196).

All People of the Book — Jews, Christian, Sabeans and Muslims — will be saved:
"Lo! Those who believe, and those who are Jews, and Sabeans, and Christians — Whosoever believeth in Allah and the Last Day and doeth right — there shall no fear come upon them neither shall they grieve" (Sura 5:69).

Salvation is only for the Muslims: Allah will accept no religion from humanity other than Islam: *"And whosoever seeks a religion other than Islam, it will not be accepted, and he will be a loser in the Hereafter"* (Sura 3:85).

"Verily, those who disbelieve in the religion of Islam, the Koran, and the Prophet Muhammad from among the people of the Scriptures and al-Mushrikun (Polytheists) will abide in the Fire of Hell. They are the worst of creatures" (Sura 98:6).

The Hadith underscores this point:

Muhammad says: *"By whom who had my soul in his hand (Allah), whoever among Jews and Christian hears my religion and dies without believing in it will go to hell fire"* (*Mishkat Al-Messabih*, vol. 1, no. 10).

A day for Allah is like a thousand years on earth: *"Verily a Day in the sight of thy Lord is like a thousand years of your reckoning"* (Sura 22:47).

A day for Allah is like fifty thousand years on earth: *"The angels and the spirit ascend unto him in a Day the measure whereof is (as) fifty thousand years"* (Sura 70:4).

The Koran was dictated word-for-word by Allah through the angel Gabriel to the prophet Muhammad; no human elements or Satanic texts are contained within it: *"Nor is it the word of the cursed Shaitan [Satan]"* (Sura 81:25).

"This Koran is not such as can be produced by other than Allah; on the contrary, it is a confirmation of [revelations] that went before it, and a fuller explanation of the Book — wherein there is no doubt — from the Lord of the worlds" (Sura 10:37).

"The revelation of the Book is from Allah, the Exalted in Power, Full of Wisdom" (Sura 45:2).

Some texts were inspired by Satan and even put into the Koran without Muhammad's knowledge: *"Never have We sent a prophet or apostle to you with whose wishes Satan did not tamper. But Allah abrogates the interjections of Satan and confirms His own revelations"* (Sura 22:52).

Jinns and men were created only to serve Allah: *"I created the jinn and humankind only that they might worship Me"* (Sura 51:56).

Some jinns and men were made for Hell: *"Many are the jinns and men we have made for Hell: They have hearts wherewith they understand not, eyes wherewith they see not, and ears wherewith they hear not. They are like cattle, nay more misguided: for they are heedless (of warning)"* (Sura 7:179).

Allah created earth, then heaven: *"He it is Who created for you all that is in the earth. Then turned He to the heaven, and fashioned it as seven heavens. And He is knower of all things"* (Sura 2:29).

Allah created heaven first, then earth: *"Are ye the harder to create, or is the heaven that He built? He raised the height thereof and ordered it; And He made dark the night thereof, and He brought forth the morn thereof. And after that He spread the earth . . ."* (Sura 79:27–30).

Jonah was cast on a naked shore: "*Then the big Fish did swallow him, and he had done acts worthy of blame. Had it not been that he (repented and) glorified Allah, He would certainly have remained inside the Fish till the Day of Resurrection. But We cast him forth on the naked shore in a state of sickness*" (Sura 37:142–145).

Allah will not forgive those who associate partners with Him: "*Allah forgiveth not that partners should be set up with Him; but He forgiveth anything else, to whom He pleaseth; to set up partners with Allah is to devise a sin Most heinous indeed*" (Sura 4:48).

Allah's words do not change: "*The word of thy Lord doth find its fulfilment in truth and in justice: None can change His words: for He is the one who heareth and knoweth all*" (Sura 6:115).

Jonah was not cast on a naked shore: "*So wait with patience for the Command of thy Lord, and be not like the Companion of the Fish, when he cried out in agony. Had not Grace from his Lord reached him, he would indeed have been cast off on the naked shore, in disgrace*" (Sura 68:48–49).

Allah will forgive those who associate partners with Him: "*The people of the Book . . . worshipped the calf even after clear signs had come to them; even so We forgave them*" (Sura 4:153).

Allah's words change: "*Whatever communications We abrogate or cause to be forgotten, We bring one better than it or like it. Do you not know that Allah has power over all things?*" (Sura 2:106).

Notes

¹ Muslim Population Statistics; muslim-canada.org/muslimstats.html

² The words *Moors* and *Saracens* are ancient terms once applied to Muslims but no longer in common use. Readers may encounter them in medieval Christian writings about Islam. Spanish Christians called the Muslims who swept in from North Africa *Moors*, and strictly speaking, the term does refer to Muslims of North Africa. (The names of two nations in Northern and Western Africa, Morocco and Mauritania, are derived from the word "Moor.") The Saracens were a tribe from Arabia. Medieval Christians began to use the word to refer to all Arab Muslims, and ultimately to all Muslims (Arab or not) who were threatening Eastern Europe from the Middle East.

³ There are numerous helpful translations of the Koran available, many of which were completed by Muslims. *The Meaning of the Glorious Koran*, a translation by the English Muslim convert Mohammed Marmaduke Pickthall, is relatively faithful to the Arabic text, although somewhat stilted in English. N. J. Dawood's *The Koran*, on the other hand, is readable in English but a less literal rendering of the Arabic. Muslims tend to dislike it because Dawood was not a Muslim. Muslims generally have high regard for *The Meaning of the Holy Qur'an* by Abdullah Yusuf Ali. It is less readable in English than Dawood's translation, and contains some quite tendentious readings of several controversial verses, but it is generally sound. As with the Bible, it is best to refer to more than one translation in order to make a serious study of the text.

⁴ Ibn Taymiyyah, "The Status of the Arabic Language in Islam," www.sunnahonline.com/ilm/quran/0021.htm.

⁵ Yusuf Islam (Cat Stevens), "How I Came to Islam," Institute of Islamic Information and Education, www.unn.ac.uk/societies/islamic/convert/17.htm.

⁶ For example, many evangelical and fundamentalist Protestants believe that one merely needs to accept Jesus as his or her "personal lord and Savior" to be saved. Nothing further is required on the part of the believer; no later sin will keep one from Heaven. This is the doctrine of *eternal security*. From a Catholic perspective, this is a little too simplistic and presumptuous. The Church has always taught that while salvation is indeed the free gift of God to be received in faith, an individual must

155

accept this gift by striving to follow the commands of Christ and by *responding* to His grace. If a person claims to have accepted Jesus and yet lives a life of serious (that is, objectively mortal) sin, it is doubtful that he or she has really accepted Jesus and His grace. Such a person is placing his or her salvation in serious jeopardy.

⁷ 1) The Early-Morning Prayer *(Fajr)*, to be prayed after dawn and before sunrise. The mu'athin proclaims, "It is better to pray than to sleep!"; 2) The Noon-Prayer *(Thuher)*; 3) The Afternoon Prayer *(Asr)*, which occurs around mid-afternoon; 4) The Evening Prayer *(Magrib)*, which is prayed during the time between the setting of the sun and the disappearance of the red sunset glow in the west; and 5) The Night Prayer *(Isha)*.

⁸ There are also numerous non-mandatory prayers in Islam. These have to do with life events:

Prayers for the dead at a funeral. These are considered to be of great importance for the soul of the deceased and are generally well attended.

Prayers for rain, for healing, and for asking a favor from Allah.

Nafela prayers, which come before and after every mandatory prayer. These are the most important non-mandatory prayers. The Nafela prayers are believed to strengthen and develop the believer's spiritual bond with Allah. They are one manifestation of Muslims' genuine attempt to observe and imitate the example of Muhammad.

⁹ "Then the prayers were enjoined on me: They were fifty prayers a day. When I returned, I passed by Moses who asked (me), What have you been ordered to do, I replied, I have been ordered to offer fifty prayers a day. Moses said, Your followers cannot bear fifty prayers a day, and by Allah, I have tested people before you, and I have tried my level best with Bani Israel [the tribes of Israel] (in vain). Go back to your Lord and ask for reduction to lessen your followers' burden. So I went back, and Allah reduced ten prayers for me. Then again I came to Moses, but he repeated the same as he had said before. Then again I went back to Allah and He reduced ten more prayers. When I came back to Moses he said the same, I went back to Allah and He ordered me to observe ten prayers a day. When I came back to Moses, he repeated the same advice, so I went back to Allah and was ordered to observe five prayers a day. When I came back to Moses, he said, What have you been ordered, I replied, I have been ordered to observe five prayers a day. He said, Your followers cannot bear five prayers a day, and no doubt, I have got an experience of the people before you, and I have tried my level best with Bani Israel, so go back to your Lord and ask for reduction to lessen your follower's burden. I said, I have requested

so much of my Lord that I feel ashamed, but I am satisfied now and surrender to Allah's Order. When I left, I heard a voice saying, I have passed My Order and have lessened the burden of My Worshippers."

[10] Muhammed Ibn Ismaiel Al-Bukhari, *Sahih al-Bukhari: The Translation of the Meanings*, trans. Muhammad M. Khan, Darussalam, Tanzania, 1997, vol. 7, book 77, no. 5927. (*Note*: this is the most important collection of the Traditions of Muhammad, the Hadith).

[11] Besides Mecca and its Ka'aba, Muslims revere Medina, the city where Muhammad fled from the pagan Quraysh in his native Mecca. It was in Medina where he established the first Islamic community. Muslim pilgrims still visit there, but it is second in importance to Mecca.

Some Muslim groups also venerate the tombs of various prophets and those Muslims consider saints. These sites can be found throughout the Muslim world. Other Muslim groups reject this practice as idol worship.

[12] Because of their close connection in the two affirmations of the Shahada, belief in Muhammad as the prophet of Allah is closely coupled with the affirmation of His unity. This unity, as attested to in Islamic tradition, involves several affirmations and negations: "The Prophet said, 'If anyone testifies that none has the right to be worshipped but Allah Alone, Who has no partners, and that Muhammad is His slave and His Messenger, and that Jesus is Allah's slave and His Messenger and His Word (Be! — and he was) which He bestowed on Mary and a Spirit created by Him, and that Paradise is the truth, and Hell is the truth, Allah will admit him into Paradise with the deeds which he had done even if those deeds were few.'"

[13] Most of these prophets are unknown today since the Koran confines itself almost completely to mentioning Biblical prophets only. Yet it says that Allah sent "messengers We have mentioned to you before and messengers We have not mentioned to you" (Sura 4:164). Although the names, nations, and eras of these prophets are not mentioned in the Koran, belief in them is required for Muslims.

Muslims believe that all prophets were sent with the same message, regardless of where they went and in what period they preached. Allah tells Muhammad, "Nothing is said to you that has not been said to other apostles before you" (Sura 41:43). However, Muslims believe that only Muhammad and his community received the message without changing it, and that the Koran is the only perfect record of the Will of Allah. All the prophets, Muslims assume, were sent to teach people how to worship Allah through prayers, almsgiving, fasting, and pilgrimages to the holy sites.

[14] The importance of angels in Islam is particularly exemplified by the

Koran's odd teachings about the angel Gabriel [*Jibreel*]. Muslims identify Gabriel, of course, as the angel who brought the Koran to Muhammad. That book calls him a "trustworthy spirit": "The Trustworthy Spirit has brought it [the Koran] down upon your [Muhammad's] heart that you may be a Warner, in the plain Arabic language" (Sura 26:193–195). Gabriel is also called "an honored messenger" (Sura 81:19), which is a title often given to the prophets themselves in the Koran; "Mighty in Power, endued with Wisdom" (Sura 53:5–6) and even "the Holy Spirit" (Sura 16:102).

¹⁵ As in the Bible, the fall of the angels in the Koran is related to the creation of Adam and Eve. But the Koran takes the substance of its teaching about the angelic fall from Jewish and Christian traditions. "Behold! We said to the angels 'Bow down to Adam': they bowed down except Iblis [Satan]. He was one of the Jinns [in the Koran these are spirit beings, either identical to or similar to angels] and he broke the command of his Lord" (Sura 18:50).

Satan disobeyed the command to bow down to Adam, according to the Koran, because he considered himself superior to men: "(Allah) said: 'What prevented you from prostrating when I commanded you?' He said: 'I am better than he: Thou didst create me from fire, and him from clay'" (Sura 7:12).

The Koran suggests an intriguing second reason why Satan refused Allah's command: he knew, somehow, that the children of Adam would do violence and would shed blood on the earth. The angels, by contrast, were doing Allah's Will, in constant praise and worship of Allah: "Behold, thy Lord said to the angels: 'I will create a viceregent on earth.' They said: 'Wilt Thou place therein one who will make mischief therein and shed blood whilst we do celebrate Thy praises and glorify Thy holy (name)?' [Allah] said: 'I know what ye know not'" (Sura 2:30).

¹⁶ Bukhari, vol. 4, book 60, no. 3409.

¹⁷ Ibn Kathir's *Commentary on the Qur'an*, Ali Baythony, Dar Al-Kutub Al-Ilmiya, Beirut, Lebanon, 1997. Vol. IV, p. 402.

¹⁸ It is very interesting to note the curious similarities that exist between Islam and Mormonism, particularly regarding the genesis of their beliefs. In both religions: 1) there was a single founder who claimed a "new" revelation; 2) there were no witnesses to or independent corroboration of this revelation; 3) there is a mix of Christian elements chosen randomly and arbitrarily; 4) both religions are somewhat carnal in their view of heaven; and 5) both allow (or allowed) polygamy.

¹⁹ "(The Prophet added), 'The angel caught me (forcefully) and pressed me so hard that I could not bear it anymore. He then released me and

again asked me to read, and I replied, 'I do not know how to read.' Thereupon he caught me again and pressed me a second time till I could not bear it anymore. He then released me and asked me again to read, but again I replied, 'I do not know how to read (or, what shall I read?).' Thereupon he caught me for the third time and pressed me and then released me and said, 'Read! In the Name of your Lord, Who has created (all that exists). Has created man from a clot. Read! And Your Lord is Most Generous . . . [unto] . . . that which he knew not' "(Sura 96:5).

[20] Bukhari, vol. 1, book 1, no. 3

[21] Ibid.

[22] Waraqa's actual full name was Waraqa bin Naufal bin Asad bin 'Abdul-'Uzza bin Qusai.

[23] Bukhari, vol. 1, book 1, no. 3.

[24] Waraqa Bin-Nawfal was not the only one who taught and inspired Muhammad. Another was a Persian, Salman Al-Farsi. Echoes of his influence can be found in the Koran and Mohammad's tradition: "(It is) a Qur'an in Arabic, without any crookedness (therein): in order that they may guard against Evil" (Sura 39:28). In Sura 16:103 Muhammad brushes aside accusations that he was taught by someone who is Persian: "we know indeed that they say, 'It is a man that teaches him.' The tongue of him they wickedly point to is notably foreign while this is Arabic, pure and clear." The Arabic word translated here as "foreign" is *A'game*, which means Persian or Iranian. The Koran's repeated insistence that it is in Arabic may betray a certain anxiety to rule out any foreign (or Persian) influence.

[25] Perhaps these Manicheans disputed with other Christian groups about the crucifixion, since the Koran presents its denial of the crucifixion as the clarification of a disputed topic: "And because of their saying: We slew the Messiah, Jesus son of Mary, Allah's messenger — they slew him not nor crucified him, but it appeared so unto them; and lo! those who disagree concerning it are in doubt thereof; they have no knowledge thereof save pursuit of a conjecture; they slew him not for certain" (Sura 4:157).

[26] " 'O people of the Book! Do ye disapprove of us for no other reason than that we believe in Allah, and the revelation that hath come to us and that which came before (us), and (perhaps) that most of you are rebellious and disobedient?' Say: 'Shall I point out to you something much worse than this, (as judged) by the treatment it received from Allah? Those who incurred the curse of Allah and His wrath, those of whom some He transformed into apes and swine, those who worshipped

evil; these are (many times) worse in rank, and far more astray from the even path!" (Sura 5:59–60).

[27] Maxime Rodinson, *Muhammad*, New York: Pantheon Books, 1971, pp. 157, 171.

[28] Sahih Muslim, book 41, no. 6985.

[29] For example, the Koran's first Sura (*Fatihah*, "The Opening") begins: "praise to Allah, the Cherisher and Sustainer of the worlds" (Sura 1:2). If Allah is the only speaker of the entire Koran, is he offering praise to himself? Muslims explain that Allah is teaching mankind this prayer, as the *Fatihah* has a status among Muslims akin to the Lord's Prayer among Christians. But this is never stated in the text.

[30] Laura Veccia Vaglieri, "The Patriarchal and Umayyad Caliphates," in *The Cambridge History of Islam*, ed. P. M. Holt, Ann K. S. Lamberton and Bernard Lewis, New York: Cambridge University Press, 1970, p. 73.

[31] Toby Lester, "What is the Koran?", *Atlantic Monthly*, January 1999. Available online at www.theatlantic.com/issues/99jan/index.htm

[32] Ibid.

[33] "But she pointed to the babe. They said: 'How can we talk to one who is a child in the cradle?' He said: 'I am indeed a servant of Allah: He hath given me revelation and made me a prophet; and He hath made me blessed wheresoever I be, and hath enjoined on me Prayer and Charity as long as I live; (He) hath made me kind to my mother, and not overbearing or miserable; so peace is on me the day I was born, the day that I die, and the day that I shall be raised up to life (again)!'" (Sura 19:29–33).

[34] See Suras 2:87; 2:136; 2:253; 3:48–51; 5:46, 110; 4:63–66; 57:27; and 61:6. He is also mentioned in lists of prophets in Suras 2:136; 3:84; 4:162; 6:85; 33:7; and 42:13.

[35] "Those messengers We endowed with gifts, some above others: To one of them Allah spoke; others He raised to degrees (of honour); to Jesus the son of Mary We gave clear (Signs), and strengthened him with the holy spirit" (Sura 2:253).

[36] See Suras 2:87, 2:253, 3:49, 3:53, 4:157, 4:171, 5:75, 5:111, 57:27, and 61:6.

[37] Sunan Abu Dawud, book 37, no. 4310.

[38] Here we can see a remarkable similarity to the words of Elizabeth in Luke 1:42, 45: "Most blessed are you among women, and blessed is the fruit of your womb. . . . Blessed are you who believed that what was spoken to you by the Lord would be fulfilled." This is most likely yet another Christian influence that seeped into Muhammad's thought.

[39] Muslim, vol. 4, book 33, no. 6429.

[40] It could be said that Islam more closely resembles Protestant Christianity in this regard than it does the Catholic faith. Though Islam has written traditions (the Hadith), it lacks an authoritative human interpreter of its accepted revelation (the Koran) when questions or disputes arise. A similar situation confronts the Protestant when he reads his Bible and seeks to understand its mysteries — he has nowhere to turn for definitive guidance. The Catholic faith, however, has always affirmed the need for such a definitive guide in matters of belief: the Magisterium (or "teaching office") of the Church. It is the Magisterium (that is, the pope and the bishops united with him) that fulfills this authoritative teaching role (see CCC 85–86, 88).

[41] Ignaz Goldhizer, a pioneering Western scholar of Hadith, gives a telling example of this: "When the Umayyad caliph 'Abd al-Malik wished to stop the pilgrimages to Mecca because he was worried lest his rival 'Abd Allah b. Zubayr should force the Syrians journeying to the holy places in Hijaz to pay him homage, he decreed that obligatory circumambulation (tawaf) could take place at the sacred place in Jerusalem with the same validity as that around the Ka'aba ordained in Islamic law. The pious theologian al-Zuhri was given the task of justifying this politically motivated reform of religious life by making up and spreading a saying traced back to the Prophet, according to which there are three mosques to which people may take pilgrimages: those in Mecca, Medina, and Jerusalem." See Ignaz Goldhizer, *Muslim studies*, vol. 2, George & Unwin Ltd., 1971, p. 45, quoted in William Van Doodewaard, "Hadith Authenticity: A Survey of Perspectives," unpub., University of Western Ontario, London, Ontario, 1996.

[42] Bukhari, vol. 4, book 59, no. 3289.

[43] Bukhari, vol. 4, book 59, no. 3295.

[44] Bukhari, vol. 4, book 59, no. 3311.

[45] Bukhari, vol. 4, book 59, no. 3322.

[46] Mishkat Al-Messabih, vol. 1, no. 119.

[47] Ibn Ishaq, *The Life of Muhammad: A Translation of Ibn Ishaq's Sirat Rasul Allah*, A. Guillaume, translator, Oxford University Press, 1955, pp. 165–166.

[48] Bukhari, vol. 1, book 8, no. 349.

[49] "Then Moses threw his rod, when, behold, it straightway swallows up all the falsehoods which they fake! Then did the sorcerers fall down, prostrate in adoration, saying: 'We believe in the Lord of the Worlds, The Lord of Moses and Aaron.' Said (Pharaoh): 'Believe ye in Him before I give you permission? Surely he is your leader, who has taught

you sorcery! But soon shall ye know! Be sure I will cut off your hands and your feet on opposite sides, and I will cause you all to die on the cross!'" (Sura 26:45–49).

⁵⁰ See Kevin Dale Miller, "What We've Learned from the Dead Sea Scrolls," *Christian Reader*, July-August 1997. Available at www.christianitytoday.com/cr/7r4/7r4036.html.

⁵¹ At the same time, however, some Islamic traditions contain bizarre anthropomorphic stories, such as this strange vision of Allah's shin in the end times: "Then the Almighty will come to them in a shape other than the one which they saw the first time, and He will say, 'I am your Lord,' and they will say, 'You are our Lord.' And none will speak to Him then but the Prophets, and then it will be said to them, 'Do you know any sign by which you can recognize Him?' They will say, 'The Shin,' and so Allah will then uncover His Shin whereupon every believer will prostrate before Him. . . ." Another focuses not on the shin only, but on the entire leg of Allah: "When Allah uncovers his leg, every Muslim, male and female will [marvel at His Beauty], and bow down in worship of His Greatness." These anthropomorphisms are often taken literally by some groups of Sunni Muslims, particularly Wahhabis.

⁵² Imam Abu Abdullah Muhammad bin Yazid Ibn-I-Maja Al-Qazwini, *Sunan Ibn-I-Majah*, trans. Muhammad Tufail Ansari, Kazi Publications, 1996, vol. 5, no. 3861.

⁵³ Barnaby Rogerson, "Trekking: All Aboard the Ship of the Desert," *Independent.co.uk*, April 15, 2000.

⁵⁴ Vatican II, *Lumen Gentium* (Dogmatic Constitution on the Church) 16; CCC 841.

⁵⁵ CCC 3.

⁵⁶ *Lumen Gentium* 1.

⁵⁷ Ibn Kathir, *Tafseer Al-Qor'an Al-Atheem*, Mohammed Ali Baythony, Dar Al-Kotob Al-Ilmiya, Beirut, 1997. Vol. 1, p. 364.

⁵⁸ Bukhari, vol. 8, book 81, no. 6526.

⁵⁹ Bukhari, vol. 4, book 60, no. 3394.

⁶⁰ "Then Adam received from his Lord words and He accepted his repentance. Lo! He is the acceptor of repentance, the Merciful" (Sura 2:37).

⁶¹ Bukhari, vol. 6, book 65, no. 4736.

⁶² In a similar vein, the Koran says that the souls of men are ever greedy: "And human inner-selves are swayed by greed. . ." (Sura 4:128). Why? If Allah created them perfectly and there is no original sin, how could the human soul be in such a state?

⁶³ Bukhari, vol. 4, book 60, no. 3431.

[64] Bukhari, vol. 3, book 33, no. 2039.

[65] These commentators are working from Sura 4:137: "Those who believe, then reject faith, then believe (again) and (again) reject faith, and go on increasing in unbelief, Allah will not forgive them nor guide them nor guide them on the way."

[66] Bukhari, vol. 9, book 87, no. 6878.

[67] As the Koran states: "Do not the Believers know, that, had Allah (so) willed, He could have guided all mankind (to the right)? But the Unbelievers: never will disaster cease to seize them for their (ill) deeds, or to settle close to their homes, until the promise of Allah come to pass, for, verily, Allah will not fail in His promise" (Sura 13:31). This idea recurs: "If We had so willed, We could certainly have brought every soul its true guidance: but the Word from Me will come true, 'I will fill Hell with Jinns [spirit beings] and men all together'" (Sura 32:13).

[68] Al-Tabrezi, *Mishkat Al-Messabih*, ed. M.N. Temem and H.N. Temem, Vol. 1, Beirut: Dar Al-Arqam Bin Al-Aqam, no. 86.

[69] Bukhari, vol. 1, book 6, no. 304.

[70] Bukhari, vol. 4, book 56, no. 2926. This oft-repeated Hadith also appears in no. 2925 and Muslim vol. 4, book 41, nos. 6981–6985.

[71] Mishkat Al-Messabih, vol. 2, no. 5552.

[72] Abu-Dawud Sulaiman bin Al-Aash'ath Al-Azdi as-Sijistani, *Sunan abu-Dawud*, Ahmad Hasan, translator, Kitab Bhavan, 1990. Book 37, no. 4310.

[73] Lists of the prophet's wives differ, but he seems to have had around twelve in all, including Hafsa, Daughter of 'Umar, who was one of his successors as the caliph, or leader of the Islamic community; Juwariya, the wife of a pagan Arab chief (Muhammad won her as the spoils of war); Raihana and Safiyya, two Jewish women whom Muhammad also won in battle; Mary the Copt, a Christian slave girl who was a gift from Al-Mokawkas, the pharaoh of Egypt (in Muhammad's new religion women could not be given as inheritances, but they evidently could be given as gifts); and Maimuna, a Meccan girl whom Muhammad married in order to secure the loyalties of two important personages: 'Amr, a Meccan chief, and Khalid bin Al-Walid, a warrior who was known as the "Sword of Allah."

[74] As the Koran states: "O Prophet! We have made lawful to thee thy wives to whom thou hast paid their dowers; and those whom thy right hand possesses [that is, slaves] out of the prisoners of war whom Allah has assigned to thee; and daughters of thy paternal uncles and aunts, and daughters of thy maternal uncles and aunts, who migrated (from Makka) with thee; and any believing woman who dedicates her

soul to the Prophet if the Prophet wishes to wed her; this only for thee, and not for the Believers (at large); We know what We have appointed for them as to their wives and the captives whom their right hands possess; in order that there should be no difficulty for thee. And Allah is Oft-Forgiving, Most Merciful" (Sura 33:50).

[75] Amnesty International, "Pakistan: Violence against women on the increase and still no protection," April 17, 2002. Available at web.amnesty.org/ai.nsf/Index/ASA330082002?OpenDocument&of= THEMES/WOMEN

[76] There is also justification from the Hadith for the use of lethal force: "Fight in the name of Allah and in the way of Allah. Fight against those who disbelieve in Allah." And "Allah's Messenger said, 'Know that Paradise is under the shades of swords [jihad in Allah's cause].'"

"To guard Muslims from infidels in Allah's Cause for one day is better than the world and whatever is on its surface. A place in Paradise as small as that occupied by the whip of one of you is better than the world and whatever is on its surface. A morning's or an evening's journey which a slave (person) travels in Allah's Cause is better than the world and whatever is on its surface."

[77] Muslim, no. 4294.

[78] Bukhari, vol. 4, book 56, no. 2941.

[79] Bat Ye'or, *The Decline of Eastern Christianity under Islam: From Jihad to Dhimmitude*, Madison, New Jersey: Fairleigh Dickinson University Press, 1996, pp. 271–272.

[80] Ibid., p. 50.

[81] Quoted in Paul Fregosi, *Jihad in the West: Muslim Conquests from the 7th to the 21st Centuries*, Buffalo, New York: Prometheus Books, 1998, pp. 84–6.

[82] Quoted in V.S. Naipaul, *Among the Believers: An Islamic Journey*, New York: Vintage Books, 1982, p. 103.

[83] Fregosi, p. 99.

[84] Fregosi, p. 119.

[85] Fregosi, p. 225.

[86] Pope Urban II, "Speech at Council of Clermont, 1095, according to Fulcher of Chartres," quoted in Bongars, *Gesta Dei per Francos*, 1, p. 382 ff., trans. in Oliver J. Thatcher, and Edgar Holmes McNeal, eds., *A Source Book for Medieval History*, New York: Scribners, 1905, 513–517. Reprinted at *Medieval Sourcebook*, www.fordham.edu/halsall/source/urban2-fulcher.html.

[87] Sunan Abu Dawud, book 14, no. 2478.

[88] Middle East Media Research Institute (MEMRI), "Leading Egyptian

Government Cleric Calls For: 'Martyrdom Attacks that Strike Horror into the Hearts of the Enemies of Allah,'" MEMRI Special Dispatch Series No. 363, April 7, 2002. www.memri.org.

[89] *Reliance of the Traveller*, o. 8.4.

[90] Anh Nga Longva, "The apostasy law in the age of universal human rights and citizenship: Some legal and political implications," The fourth Nordic conference on Middle Eastern Studies: The Middle East in globalizing world, Oslo, 13–16 August 1998, www.hf.uib.no/smi/pao/longva.html.

[91] Muslim, vol. 3, book 17, no. 4206.

[92] Bukhari, vol. 4, book 56, no. 3053.

[93] Ahmed ibn Naqib al-Misri, *Reliance of the Traveller: A Classic Manual of Islamic Sacred Law*, translated by Nuh Ha Mim Keller. Amana Publications, 1999, p. xx.

[94] *Reliance of the Traveller*, o. 11.5.

[95] Similarly, the culture of India has been profoundly shaped by Hindu beliefs. For example, belief in the doctrines of reincarnation and karma have led to an acceptance of poverty in Indian society: the man starving in the street is there because of "bad karma" in his previous life. It should be clear that such beliefs adversely affect the progress and development of a society.

Occasionally, some non-Catholics make similar assertions about certain poor Catholic countries such as Mexico, Brazil, and even Ireland. It has been asserted that such countries are impoverished due to "Catholic Church oppression" and a lack of the "Protestant work ethic." An objective study of history, however, demonstrates that socialist and imperialist (and not ecclesiastical) oppression are the real culprits responsible for the poor socioeconomic condition of these nations.

[96] Amir Taheri, *The Spirit of Allah: Khomeini and the Islamic Revolution*, Adler and Adler, 1986, pp. 20, 45.

[97] Ibid., p. 44.

[98] "When if one of them receiveth tidings of the birth of a female, his face remaineth darkened, and he is wroth inwardly. He hideth himself from the folk because of the evil of that whereof he hath had tidings, (asking himself): Shall he keep it in contempt, or bury it beneath the dust. Verily evil is their judgment" (Sura 16:58–59).

[99] Within these teachings, though, lies a critical philosophical problem: the soul is *spiritual*. Unlike the body, the human soul, being a spirit, has no parts because it has no matter — in other words, it cannot be divided because it has nothing *to* divide. Catholic belief recognizes this by teaching that all human souls are created directly and immediately

by God at the moment of conception. In teaching that men and women were created from a single soul, Islam contradicts sound logic; this belief seems to be a corruption of the Genesis creation account in which the *body* of Eve is formed from a part of Adam's *body*, that is, a rib (Gn 2:21–23). No "division of soul" is mentioned.

[100] See Christopher Dickey and Rod Nordland, "The Fire That Won't Die Out," *Newsweek*, July 22, 2002, pp. 34–37.

[101] Quoted in Muhammad Ali Al-Hashimi, *The Ideal Muslimah: The True Islamic Personality of the Muslim Woman as Defined in the Qur'an and Sunnah*, International Islamic Publishing House, 1998.

[102] See "Update: Court Rejects Saadawi Forcible Divorce Case," Women Living Under Muslim Laws, August 1, 2001, www.wluml.org/english/alerts/2001/egypt/egypt-saadawi.htm. The idea that a third party can force a couple to divorce due to the apostasy of one of the spouses is known as *hisba* in Islamic law.

[103] Bukhari, vol. 7, book 67, no. 5206.

[104] Ahmed ibn Naqib al-Misri, *Reliance of the Traveller: A Classic Manual of Islamic Sacred Law*, (*'Umdat al-Salik*), trans. Nuh Ha Mim Keller. Amana Publications, 1999, o. 24.8.

[105] See also Bukhari, vol. 3, book 52, no. 2661.

[106] *Reliance*, o. 24.9.

[107] *Reliance*, p. xx.

[108] See Sisters in Islam, "Rape, Zina, and Incest," April 6, 2000, www.muslimtents.com/sistersinislam/resources/sdefini.htm.

[109] Quoted in Mark Goldblatt, "Why the West Is Better," *New York Post*, January 30, 2002.

[110] Sunan Abu Dawud, book 32, no. 4092.

Appendix

*Declaration on the Relation of the Church
To Non-Christian Religions*

NOSTRA AETATE

Proclaimed by His Holiness
Pope Paul VI
On October 28, 1965
(Second Vatican Council)

1. In our time, when day by day mankind is being drawn closer together, and the ties between different peoples are becoming stronger, the Church examines more closely her relationship to non-Christian religions. In her task of promoting unity and love among men, indeed among nations, she considers above all in this declaration what men have in common and what draws them to fellowship.

One is the community of all peoples, one their origin, for God made the whole human race to live over the face of the earth.[1] One also is their final goal, God. His providence, His manifestations of goodness, His saving design extend to all men,[2] until that time when the elect will be united in the Holy City, the city ablaze with the glory of God, where the nations will walk in His light.[3]

Men expect from the various religions answers to the unsolved riddles of the human condition, which today, even as in former times, deeply stir the hearts of men: What is man? What is the meaning, the aim of our life? What is moral good, what sin? Whence suffering and what purpose does it serve? Which is the road to true happiness? What are death, judgment and retribution after death? What, finally, is that ultimate inexpressible mystery which encompasses our existence: whence do we come, and where are we going?

2. From ancient times down to the present, there is found among various peoples a certain perception of that hidden power which hovers over the course of things and over the events of human history; at times some indeed have come to the recognition of a Supreme Being, or even of a Father. This perception and recognition penetrates their lives with a profound religious sense.

Religions, however, that are bound up with an advanced culture have struggled to answer the same questions by means of more refined concepts and a more developed language. Thus in Hinduism, men contemplate the divine mystery and express it through an inexhaustible abundance of myths and through searching philosophical inquiry. They seek freedom from the anguish of our human condition either through ascetical practices or profound meditation or a flight to God with love and trust. Again, Buddhism, in its various forms, realizes the radical insufficiency of this changeable world; it teaches a way by which men, in a devout and confident spirit, may be able either to acquire the state of perfect liberation, or attain, by their own efforts or through higher help, supreme illumination. Likewise, other religions found everywhere try to counter the restlessness of the human heart, each in its own manner, by proposing "ways," comprising teachings, rules of life, and sacred rites. The Catholic Church rejects nothing that is true and holy in these religions. She regards with sincere reverence those ways of conduct and of life, those precepts and teachings which, though differing in many aspects from the ones she holds and sets forth, nonetheless often reflect a ray of that Truth which enlightens all men. Indeed, she proclaims, and ever must proclaim Christ "the way, the truth, and the life"

(John 14:6), in whom men may find the fullness of religious life, in whom God has reconciled all things to Himself.[4]

The Church, therefore, exhorts her sons, that through dialogue and collaboration with the followers of other religions, carried out with prudence and love and in witness to the Christian faith and life, they recognize, preserve and promote the good things, spiritual and moral, as well as the socio-cultural values found among these men.

3. The Church regards with esteem also the Moslems. They adore the one God, living and subsisting in Himself; merciful and all-powerful, the Creator of heaven and earth,[5] *who has spoken to men; they take pains to submit wholeheartedly to even His inscrutable decrees, just as Abraham, with whom the faith of Islam takes pleasure in linking itself, submitted to God. Though they do not acknowledge Jesus as God, they revere Him as a prophet. They also honor Mary, His virgin Mother; at times they even call on her with devotion. In addition, they await the day of judgment when God will render their deserts to all those who have been raised up from the dead. Finally, they value the moral life and worship God especially through prayer, almsgiving and fasting.*

Since in the course of centuries not a few quarrels and hostilities have arisen between Christians and Moslems, this sacred synod urges all to forget the past and to work sincerely for mutual understanding and to preserve as well as to promote together for the benefit of all mankind social justice and moral welfare, as well as peace and freedom [emphasis added].

4. As the sacred synod searches into the mystery of the Church, it remembers the bond that spiritually ties the people of the New Covenant to Abraham's stock.

Thus the Church of Christ acknowledges that, according to God's saving design, the beginnings of her faith and her election are found already among the Patriarchs, Moses and the prophets. She professes that all who believe in Christ —

Abraham's sons according to faith[6] — are included in the same Patriarch's call, and likewise that the salvation of the Church is mysteriously foreshadowed by the chosen people's exodus from the land of bondage. The Church, therefore, cannot forget that she received the revelation of the Old Testament through the people with whom God in His inexpressible mercy concluded the Ancient Covenant. Nor can she forget that she draws sustenance from the root of that well-cultivated olive tree onto which have been grafted the wild shoots, the Gentiles.[7] Indeed, the Church believes that by His cross Christ, Our Peace, reconciled Jews and Gentiles. making both one in Himself.[8]

The Church keeps ever in mind the words of the Apostle about his kinsmen: "theirs is the sonship and the glory and the covenants and the law and the worship and the promises; theirs are the fathers and from them is the Christ according to the flesh" (Rom. 9:4–5), the Son of the Virgin Mary. She also recalls that the Apostles, the Church's main-stay and pillars, as well as most of the early disciples who proclaimed Christ's Gospel to the world, sprang from the Jewish people.

As Holy Scripture testifies, Jerusalem did not recognize the time of her visitation,[9] nor did the Jews in large number, accept the Gospel; indeed not a few opposed its spreading.[10] Nevertheless, God holds the Jews most dear for the sake of their Fathers; He does not repent of the gifts He makes or of the calls He issues — such is the witness of the Apostle.[11] In company with the Prophets and the same Apostle, the Church awaits that day, known to God alone, on which all peoples will address the Lord in a single voice and "serve him shoulder to shoulder" (Soph. 3:9).[12]

Since the spiritual patrimony common to Christians and Jews is thus so great, this sacred synod wants to foster and recommend that mutual understanding and respect which is the fruit, above all, of biblical and theological studies as well as of fraternal dialogues.

True, the Jewish authorities and those who followed their lead pressed for the death of Christ;[13] still, what happened in His passion cannot be charged against all the Jews, without distinction, then alive, nor against the Jews of today. Although the Church is the new people of God, the Jews should not be presented as rejected or accursed by God, as if this followed from the Holy Scriptures. All should see to it, then, that in catechetical work or in the preaching of the word of God they do not teach anything that does not conform to the truth of the Gospel and the spirit of Christ.

Furthermore, in her rejection of every persecution against any man, the Church, mindful of the patrimony she shares with the Jews and moved not by political reasons but by the Gospel's spiritual love, decries hatred, persecutions, displays of anti-Semitism, directed against Jews at any time and by anyone.

Besides, as the Church has always held and holds now, Christ underwent His passion and death freely, because of the sins of men and out of infinite love, in order that all may reach salvation. It is, therefore, the burden of the Church's preaching to proclaim the cross of Christ as the sign of God's all-embracing love and as the fountain from which every grace flows.

5. We cannot truly call on God, the Father of all, if we refuse to treat in a brotherly way any man, created as he is in the image of God. Man's relation to God the Father and his relation to men his brothers are so linked together that Scripture says: "He who does not love does not know God" (1 John 4:8).

No foundation therefore remains for any theory or practice that leads to discrimination between man and man or people and people, so far as their human dignity and the rights flowing from it are concerned.

The Church reproves, as foreign to the mind of Christ, any discrimination against men or harassment of them because of their race, color, condition of life, or religion. On the contrary, following in the footsteps of the holy Apostles Peter and Paul, this sacred synod ardently implores the Christian faithful to "maintain good fellowship among the nations" (1 Peter 2:12), and, if possible, to live for their part in peace with all men,[14] so that they may truly be sons of the Father who is in heaven.[15]

NOTES

[1] Cf. Acts 17:26

[2] Cf. Wis. 8:1; Acts 14:17; Rom. 2:6–7; 1 Tim. 2:4

[3] Cf. Apoc. 21:23f.

[4] Cf. 2 Cor. 5:18–19

[5] Cf. St. Gregory VII, letter XXI to Anzir (Nacir), King of Mauritania (Pl. 148, col. 450f.)

[6] Cf. Gal. 3:7

[7] Cf. Rom. 11:17–24

[8] Cf. Eph. 2:14–16

[9] Cf. Lk. 19:44

[10] Cf. Rom. 11:28

[11] Cf. Rom. 11:28–29; cf. dogmatic Constitution, *Lumen Gentium* (Light of nations) AAS, 57 (1965) p. 20

[12] Cf. Is. 66:23; Ps. 65:4; Rom. 11:11–32

[13] Cf. John 19:6

[14] Cf. Rom. 12:18

[15] Cf. Matt. 5:45

Index

About the Authors

Daniel Ali is a Catholic convert from Islam. After many years of study and reflection, Daniel was led to the foot of the Cross — to the realization that the God of the Universe desires an intimate relationship with man and that He did, in fact, send His Son to dwell among us. Daniel was received into the Catholic Church by Father William G. Most in 1998. Daniel has gained national note as the founder of the Christian-Islamic Forum as well as his Video series with Father Mitch Pacwa, S.J., the host of *EWTN Live!* Today he travels throughout the world leading seminars on Islam. Daniel and his wife live in Virginia. He can be reached at Daniel@ChristianIslamicForum.org.

Robert Spencer began his study of Islam in 1980 when he first read the Koran at the invitation of Palestinian and Saudi Muslims. This initial interest was fueled by his grandparents' unique history as Christians who were raised under the last great Muslim empire, the Ottoman Empire, and who immigrated to the United States in 1919. Spencer is the author of two previous books on Islam, *Islam Unveiled: Disturbing Questions About the World's Fastest Growing Faith* (San Francisco: Encounter Books, 2002), which quickly became a best-seller, and an in-depth study of jihad, *Onward Muslim Soldiers: How Jihad Still Threatens America and the West* (Washington, D.C.: Regnery Publishing, 2003). He can be reached at spencer952@hotmail.com.